Because of You

By
Jacquelyn Longobardo

It Is Written Publishers Inc. – Life Experiences Ministry LLC

It Is Written Publishers Inc.

P.O. Box 722

Dobbs Ferry, New York 10502

ISBN: 9781543941319

Library of Congress Control Number: 2018908547

First edition published July 2018

Book Cover & Design by
Elizabeth Martland, SoundviewSonic Designs

CONTENTS

DEDICATION

This book is dedicated to God, my all mighty Father, to the agreement I made with Him, and to the most amazing relationship that I have with Him and with Jesus Christ. I wrote this book, not for myself, but because He told me that He wanted me to share it with others. I had no idea how to write a book, much less share my personal life, but I trusted Him to guide me page by page, chapter by chapter, and to provide the right people to enter my life to make it happen. I'm sharing this with you because I love Him and His people with all my heart. I love my family, my one and only son, Beau, and every friend God has blessed me with along the way. I've forgiven those who came against me and with a gracious heart I've survived every trial put before me. Now, as an ordained minister, I've committed my life to delivering His people from emotional damage and helping to transform their lives into lives of freedom and joy. That doesn't mean that my own journey ends there, I'm human and still have my life to live, problems to face, and weaknesses to improve on. I'm not above what may come my way; life is hard sometimes, but with faith, trust and by partnering with Jesus Christ, everything works out through His grace, and in His time.

Because of God, I know everything is possible. Because of Him, I know all things can be overcome. Because of Him, I know my life has meaning, and what I once thought was small, was part of a much larger purpose.

I also dedicate this book to my loving parents, Carolyn and Jack Centonze who guided me, yet allowed me to make my own mistakes. It's clear to me that God knew that they were exactly the right parents for me.

INTRODUCTION

"Something happened on the day of your birth. A bit of sunlight slipped to earth, and scattered its rays on the days we'd know, and glazed each one with a gentle glow. And all these years – in pleasure and strife – your light and your smile have graced my life. And so, on your birthday I celebrate, too; for so much of my joy was born with you." 1

"To my Jacquelyn,

In my mind's eye I can fly back in time and still see you as a perfect little doll. You were so cute, and I loved you so much. I remember playing hide and seek with you for hours on end. You'd run and hide and laugh so much each time you were found. I remember so many magical moments as you were growing into an elegant young lady. I remember the fun and laughter of your school years and the happiness you and your friends brought into my life. I watched you grow into a very mature woman right before my eyes. Sometimes I'm amazed at the wonder of it. I marvel at your ability to care while raising our terrific little boy (Beau) my grandson.

You know motherhood is the most important work on earth. Through Beau I still can be transported into the wonderful world of childhood (thank you). Jacquelyn, I find you to be quite remarkable and I'm proud to be your Mom. I love you. Kisses. Hugs. Laugh. Smile. Be happy. Enjoy. Treat yourself good. Sing. Dance. Go roller blading. This card says exactly what's in my heart. – Happy Birthday, Mom (1997)."

Today is September 5th and I'm in the final phases of finishing this book, having worked on it for much longer than expected. Life continuously got in the way, and my frustrations in not getting it done really bothered me and weighed heavily on my spirit. But God kept putting me back on track, encouraging, insisting and finally allowing me to complete it. I didn't realize until now, that it wasn't just about recounting my past and sharing lessons learned, but that this book had its own path that needed to be taken, that what I thought was the most important chapters weren't; that what I thought were the most important topics may have been the least; that life had to occur during its journey to bring me through a deeper understanding that God indeed was in it and leading me to the conclusion. It was in His timing that this was written, not necessarily mine.

This past Friday, looking for a particular picture and sorting through bins in my closet, I found a birthday card from my mother. It was as if I had never seen it before. Fourteen years ago today, my mother left this physical world and went to her heavenly home to be with God. I love her for watching over me growing up, and now, as I finish these writings. I hope our words bless you, as much as sharing them has blessed me.

[1] Quote by Robert Sexton; Blue Mountain Arts

CHAPTER 1
IT'S ALL ABOUT RELATIONSHIPS

"We know that in all things God works for the good of those who love him, who have been called according to his purpose." Romans 8:28 , NIV

God puts wonderful people in our lives; He also allows dark ones and some not so great ones to pass through. But, He gives us the armor to protect ourselves against those that rise against us. He continuously and unconditionally gives us the opportunity to forge a bond and relationship with Him, with Jesus and with the Holy Spirit; relationships and bonds that cannot be broken and ones that can get us through anything and anyone. Physical and emotional battles; addictions, violence, sickness, abuse; they can all be overcome through our relationship with Him.

We're connected to each other through families, mutual friends, jobs, churches, neighborhoods; there are so many ways that we often don't even realize the magnitude. Our lives are built around relationships and influenced by the people that we allow to come in and out. Everyone has a purpose. Even the bad ones. There are traumatic trials we go through, and while they may be difficult, it's often those trials that push us closer to or away from God. Within the journey of our lives, because of God's grace, He aligns the most significant, beautiful people to help us and join our journey when we need them the most. He gave me a loving family and wonderful friends that allowed me to live, laugh, love, fail and succeed; but always stood by me. Because I cherish all my relationships, I've never given up, and I will continue to love, live, and enjoy each one and endure through whatever comes my way.

My friend, Emel and I were initially from two very different worlds. I was raised in the Bronx, in a Catholic home, my life revolved around church, Jesus, friends, and family; a dysfunctional family, but one full of love. I was a happy, outgoing kid and loved Jesus, loved people and loved my family, and I knew that my parents and Jesus loved me.

Emel was raised in Turkey in a Moslem home by her mother and grandparents. Her mother, an interpreter at an Air Force base, remarried an American stationed there, and at the age of six, they moved to the U.S. and left her grandparents behind. Her strong family foundation crumbled, she no longer felt loved or had the family comfort that she once had. Not fully understanding the language, the culture, and being painfully shy, she stayed to herself and found her comfort in God.

Despite our childhood differences growing up, we found that in our teen and adult years, we had followed similar paths, parallel experiences, and half way through these writings, we found that our paths had crossed. Unknowingly, some of our actions had even altered and affected the other's life. We had been in the same room, sat in the same chair, climbed up and down the same ladder stocking shelves; found out we were pregnant a few months apart and had never even met. As I drove out, she may very well have passed me driving in. She ended up trying

2

to save what I had helped build; both of us walking away from a failed business and eventually failed marriages. About nine years later, we met for the first time at work, an investment firm in Greenwich, Connecticut. Sitting four desks apart, we instantly bonded as if we had known each other forever; not realizing how close we had come so many times before.

God works in amazing ways. Looking back at our lives, we now understand that there were no mistakes or coincidences in our personal journeys, or in our intertwined paths. It was by His grand design that we were to end up at the same point at the same time, with the same life's lessons, and look back knowing that everything we endured was for a reason.

After I received my calling, I knew there was much to do to become a minister, I had a lot to learn and needed to find a way to establish myself. Emel has always been a writer and determined to get her college degree in Journalism or Creative Writing; but life gave her two amazing daughters that she had to put through college first. Though we always stayed connected, we had our personal goals to achieve. Ten years into our friendship, I became ordained and she finished her degree. God kept us together for a greater purpose – His.

I knew I had to write this book but had no idea how or even where to begin. He gave me a writer that understood everything I went through, because she went through the same wonderful things, the same heartaches, and the same pain that comes with abusive relationships. We both knew that while we experienced love, loss, pain and the trials in our lives, we came through it stronger because of Him; sometimes broken, often wondering why and questioning His reasons; eventually under-standing that God's grace aligns the right people at the right time and for the right purpose.

We live in a physical world that's broken, a world where both good and evil exist, but there is a spiritual battle going on in the unseen. However, God has equipped us to overcome every evil and He will deliver us through it and be-yond it. This is really something we need to understand.

We are not alone; never have been and never will be as long as we embrace and grow in our relationship with God. While this is a story of my life, it's not meant to be a memoir. Sharing my private life isn't easy, but by sharing it, I hope it will demonstrate to someone going through similar situations that life isn't always easy, but you don't have to stay stuck. All that I experienced in my life, I had to experience to be able to teach it now. Everything was necessary to achieve the purpose that He had for me. Nothing was wasted! Emel agreed to help me write my journey from childhood to becoming ordained. But, she insisted that for me to truly write about my past in a way that would make a difference to someone reading it, I had to not only relive the memories, but go back to the places that changed my life. She promised that she would be right there with me.

My family's apartment was still as I remembered it. The four-story, stucco building, with its brick front and dormer windows jutting out from the roofline hadn't changed much.

CHAPTER 2
HUMBLE BEGINNINGS

"Your beginning will seem humble, so
prosperous will your future be." Job 8:7, NIV

Life for me began in the Bronx, but was built, fragmented, and flourished through the predominately Italian Catholic neighborhoods of Yonkers, Mt. Vernon and Dobbs Ferry, New York. Emel met me at my apartment and we headed out on our first, of many days, in retracing the steps of my life. I didn't really think it was going to be helpful given that everything I wanted to write about was already forever etched heavily in my mind and in my heart. But, I decided it couldn't hurt, and she was pretty adamant; plus, since she agreed to help me write this, she felt it would also help her to see where I grew up. Though I live only a few miles away now, I hadn't returned to the old neighborhood in years.

It was the first few weeks of spring and promised to be 65 degrees, sunny and beautiful. The morning was chilly; and the air was refreshing, but apprehension mixed with nerves, and the excitement of returning to what I had once called home, was starting to creep in. Exiting off the Bronx River Parkway, we drove under the raised train tracks that run along the avenues. Stores lined both sides of the street and in every nook a clothing shop or hardware store; an Italian bakery, Spanish grocer, or Jamaican restaurant. The energy of the day started building in my chest. Turning down Nereid Avenue and taking a left onto Furman, my childhood memories came flooding back. I felt comforted going back to the old neighborhood. I loved those years. I loved my family and friends, and the way I grew up, playing on the street. We were always out doing something; barreling down the street in sleds during winter or riding bikes in the summer; I really loved it.

We parked in front of a two-story, red brick building with an arched doorway, the black metal numbers, 4428, still on the white door; the home of my first childhood friend. A little worn for its years, but still had a comforting feel to it, even with the small aluminum sign with the NYPD shield that read "Attention. Patrolled by NYPDs "Operation Clean Halls."

Across the street, my family's apartment was still as I remembered it. The four-story, stucco building, with its brick front and dormer windows jutting out from the roof line hadn't changed much. Except for the peeling paint on the battleship gray concrete steps and the fading mustardy yellow paint someone had applied to the stucco, it was still the same. Out of a small patch of weeds at the bottom of the steps, looking out of place, almost forgotten, grew a struggling pink climbing rose that I imagine someone's grandmother must have planted years ago. It wound itself up the handrail and tried climbing the wall that supported it; the thorns made it impossible for anyone walking up to hold on. I had lived in the attic apartment with my parents, and my younger sister and brother. While we weren't materially rich, we were love rich.

"Em! It's almost like it was when I lived here!"

I couldn't believe it. The neighborhood was almost exactly the way it was when we left it over forty years ago. I could envision the families that lived within steps of each other; the older people sitting on chairs on the stoop watching the kids playing on the sidewalk; and my mom's red station wagon parked on the street. There was no sense of who had what, how big your yard was or how much money you had or didn't have. Our family was like every other family - dysfunctional. Despite my dad's alcoholism, and my mother working hard to raise us, they created a home filled with love and understanding. Their life was hard, but they loved us, and we knew it.

My mother and grandmother always called me Sunshine.

CHAPTER 3
CHILDLIKE FAITH

"Let the children come to me; do not hinder them, for to such belongs the kingdom of God. Truly, I say to you, whoever does not receive the kingdom of God like a child shall not enter it...And he took them in his arms and blessed them, laying his hands on them." Mark 10:14-16, ESV

Growing up in the 60's, families were families – dads went to work, moms stayed home, the kids went to school, came home and played outside until it was time to come in for dinner. My world revolved around church, friends and my family; everyone and everything, all within a few blocks. At five years old, I already knew Jesus. Sitting in the pew during mass, I believed that out of all these people, I loved Him the most. I could feel His presence close and felt incredibly special that He chose me to love. I lived each day treating people the way He would want me to; with kindness, compassion and warmth.

While my days were full of light and warmth, dark dreams came with the cloak of night. No one ever explained to me that the Devil really existed. My family and the nuns in my school always seemed to mention, rather than elaborate, on what evil really was. As a child, I was terrified to go to sleep. A wolf and visions of evil forces swirled above my head. Every night, it was the same nightmare. I would find myself running through the darkness, the grass, tall, and the enemy fast. I knew if he caught me, he would hurt me, so I would run as fast as I could toward home, breathless and scared to death, but I would keep going. The wolf always closed in on me, his fangs sharp; he was faster and stronger, and he would pounce and wrestle me to the ground. His paws were tremendous; and as he tried to maul me to death, I would gasp for air trying to fight him off. I would scream myself awake, and my little feet would hit the ground and I would run through the dark apartment and jump into my parent's bed for safety.

Every night the same dream. Every night I ran across our apartment to my parent's room, terrified. As a child, I was happy; exceptionally bubbly and loving. I felt so blessed in my relationship with Jesus; He was the big brother I never had and always wanted. I felt like He loved me so much that I shined. But every night, I feared the wolf. I loved being in the warmth of the sunshine, outside playing, but as soon as dusk started setting in, I'd get that sinking feeling. My heart raced with panic knowing it would soon be time to go to sleep. I hoped and prayed each night that this night would be different.

My little sister's bed was right next to mine. How did she do it? How did she just fall asleep? She said, "Just do what I do, make believe your dreams are like a TV, when a bad one comes, just change the channel." I said I would try it. But as I watched her nod off to sleep, I noticed the long fringes on the brown and white vest hanging over our bedroom door. Though my grandmother had lovingly crocheted it for me, the shadows began to look like wolf claws on the walls. The room grew darker and my fear grew deeper. Frozen stiff, scared, and looking up at the ceiling, I wondered if I should just start running to my parent's room rather than going to sleep and living through the nightmare again.

My father would once again walk me around the apartment with a flashlight, reassuring me that there wasn't a wolf in the house. Tucking me in, he would comfort me.

"Maybe you should just try to sleep Pal?" He'd kiss me goodnight and go back to his room. Then it happened. The angel came.

"Mom! Mom! Mom! Come here!" I yelled loud enough and long enough to wake her. She came running into my room.

"The angel is here," I whispered.

"What are you talking about?" she asked. "What angel? Where?"

"Right there above my head, up on the ceiling." I pointed to show her. She looked at the ceiling.

"I don't see anything," she said. "No, Mom." I was steadfast and certain. "The angel is here."

"Well, what do you see?" She asked, "Are they like little angels, with wings flying with harps?"

"No!" I cried.

"Well, what do they look like then?"

"It's my Guardian Angel." I whispered in awe.

No one had ever explained this to me, yet those were the words that came out of my mouth.   Everyone has a guardian angel; and mine was above me. Its face was a perfect oval shape and shined as if a lamp were giving out light through the top of a lamp shade onto the ceiling; except there were no lamps on. The light of the angel was bright and circular. It had movement, like the mirage that rises from the road in front of you on a hot summer day. It never went outside of its perfect shape.

The enemy always wants us to live in fear, but he has no authority over us. We just give him the power over us when we put our thoughts and our emotions into it. *"For God has not given us a spirit of fear and timidity, but of power, love, and self-discipline." Timothy 2 1:7.*

We are in control of our choices, decisions and emotions. God didn't give us a spirit of fear; fear comes from the enemy. He gave us a spirit with power! He gave us a spirit of love and self-discipline that lives and dwells inside of us – He gave us His Holy Spirit to counsel us.

By the time I got to first grade, the one thing that I knew for sure, was that I loved Jesus. He protected me, and He was real. The other thing I knew for sure, was that the devil also existed. But God had sent His Only Son, Jesus to defeat the devil and sent His angels to watch over me. I would always have victory over the plots of the enemy. Why me God? Why? Why did

I need to experience and understand the extremes of good and evil at such a young age? I was just a child. God knew the answer. He gave me the gift of discernment to distinguish the motives in people's hearts. It was to protect me and others.

My mother always thought it was strange when I told her the outcome of a situation before it even happened. I've never been wrong, even when I desperately wanted to be. I have always squelched seeing the bad, and focused on seeing the good in people, especially in relationships and matters of the heart. But the discerning spirit has always shown me the motive behind hearts, the good, as well as the evil, and how people manipulate to achieve their own agendas. It happens in job settings, corporations, governments, politics, churches, families, and relationships.

As I grew up, I would experience that despite being able to see the evil in the hearts of others, I would try to find a way to like a person by looking for the good. I tried to analyze what made them that way and showed them love. This didn't always turn out in my best interest! I've been known to hang on to relationships a lot longer than I should have. But I truly felt and hoped that by showing someone love and patience that it could change or help them.

So, why me God? Why now, middle-aged, have you called me to share my personal, private life? I've been hurt so badly, things didn't always work out the way I wanted them to.

I haven't always changed others; I've made plenty of my own mistakes and wrong turns along the way.

In my heart and mind; in that deep, deep core of my spirit and being, I heard "Because you know Me. It's because of our relationship that you got through it all. Others didn't see your pain the way that I did, yet you showed them love, happiness, and joy even when you were in your hardest of trials. That was My love, My joy and My tears. It's Me they saw in you My daughter. It's Me who got you through it all. We did it together. It's Me who wants you to tell your story. Even what seemed to have not worked out back then, is not wasted. It's meant to be learned from; to refine and mature you. I've built a strong in faith, yet humble, loving character in you. Going through the hard times made you compassionate and understanding so you could help others. It's not just your story, it's our story to give hope to My people, to deliver them out of their bondage, to set them free with the future and plans that I have for them."

"Okay God, I'm Yours. I love You with all my heart, my soul and my strength. I love You and I love who You love. I'll do it – I promise You – I'll do it." Always having felt different, I grew closer to God. He was real; there was never a question in my mind or my heart. Despite the nightmares and visions, my mother and grandmother always called me Sunshine. They would tease me and tell me to walk out of the room and come back in. When I walked back in, they would smile and say "See the room just got so much brighter, just like sunshine!" Have you ever had a nightmare or a bad dream as a child and screamed out for your parent? Maybe you went running to find them for comfort, knowing that you could trust them to hold and protect you.

"Em, as a child I didn't wake from an alarming dream and contemplate not being comforted. All I knew was that I was scared; really scared and I ran as fast as I could to my parents and trusted that they would be there. That's what childlike faith is. It's not being or acting like a child; it's going to God right away with urgency."

When I ran to my parent's room with my heart racing, they didn't question or judge me before they comforted me. They didn't hold it against me that my homework wasn't done, or if I had done something that day that upset or angered them. They comforted me unconditionally. We sometimes think that we must be perfect, or we've sinned and therefore have lost our right or connection to God to seek His comfort. But it's completely the opposite! He wants you to run to Him; He wants to comfort you. He is the perfect parent.

Child-like faith is knowing that you can trust Him to guard, protect, comfort, heal, and provide for and love you. It's not trying to brave it all by yourself in your own understanding. He promises that if you have the faith of a child you will enter His Kingdom. Don't waste time or worry that you haven't done everything right. It's never too late to trust Him. He's always waiting for you to call out His name because He longs to help you and to have a relationship with you.

CHAPTER 4
GOD IS REAL, BUT SO IS THE ENEMY

*"Be alert and of sober mind. Your enemy the
devil prowls around like a roaring lion looking
for someone to devour." 1 Peter 5:8, NIV*

Looking up at the dormer windows on the side, I remembered that the bathroom was under one window, and the stove and kitchen sink under the other. My parent's room was in the front of the apartment overlooking the street with a window next to their bed. I used to be able to stand on the floor and touch the top of the pane. Life was wonderful for the first three years of my life here. I had my parent's all to myself. The house was neat and clean, just the way I liked things. Perfect.

March 10th, 1966, all that changed. My grandmother and I were playing on our kitchen floor, pretending to drink milk out of tea cups, from the plastic carton I took out of my little toy, refrigerator. It had pictures of food on the inside door; we were having a wonderful time together. At that moment, my parents walked in with TWO babies. Where did these babies come from!?

"Jacquelyn, this is your new baby brother and sister."

I was so upset! TWO babies! And their birthday was a week before mine. My very Italian grandmother, whom I loved dearly, was a seamstress and made all our clothes match. We looked like triplets! I don't remember ever having my own birthday cake after that. It was always a cake for three.

We started off with very humble beginnings in our apartment. My mother had to carry the twins down three flights of stairs, one under each arm like footballs, and would motion "Move, move!" for me to go first. As I got old enough to go outside by myself, which I always tried to do, my mother would call out, "Take the twins with you!" Couldn't they find their own friends? I tried to wiggle out of it all the time. They were more interested in finding spiders and bugs, and playing S.W.A.T. in the mud, while I wanted to play Millionaire. We were very different, but our parent's message of love and family importance remained the same.

The room I shared with the twins faced the backyard and the raised tracks of the L-train. As I stood reminiscing, the train sped by grumbling, rattling and shaking the rails under its force. One summer, we found a reddish brown, shepherd mix dog under the tracks. We pleaded with my mother to please, pretty please let us keep her for just one night. One night turned into years, but that was our dog – Precious – we loved her!

"Hey, we're being watched" Em whispered.

Two ladies, probably in their 70's, were sitting on the porch next door on blue and green strapped lawn chairs, the kind that would stick to you and leave waffle marks on your legs when you got up. Whispering to each other, they gave us a look to let us know that they were watching us.

I laughed, "We better introduce ourselves before they call for reinforcements!"

I didn't know them back then, they had moved to the block around the time we left. We talked about a typical Saturday and how the kids would run outside and call for friends. On cold days we'd sit in the lobby of the buildings and play jacks. They said that there weren't too many kids left on the block, but that they remembered how they built igloos and forts in the snow and slid down icy driveways so hard that they slammed into the garage doors. I asked them about the two boys that used to live next door; they said one had joined the army and the other was working in the city. I mentioned Charlie, who used to live in the apartment building on the corner; he was bad news.

"He was a drug dealer," one nodded as the other one confirmed.

"There was another family at the other end of the block; one of the wealthiest in the neighborhood. They had the nic-est house and a pool. Later, we found out that they were co-caine dealers" I explained. They remembered them too.

"Their oldest girl was beautiful but got involved with one of the guys down the block. She married him and ended up getting pretty messed up," the other one replied.

I had known her growing up, she turned every guy's head. She was sweet and drop dead gorgeous. It was a shame to hear that she chose to marry a violent drug addict, and the life that she ended up having. The neighborhood was good if you stayed good – but there was trouble lurking if you wanted to venture in that direction – and you didn't have to venture very far.

"Em, it all stems from Satan, the enemy, the father of lies. His only mission is to take away joy, ruin lives, destroy and kill. He preys on weaknesses."

Trouble is so easy to get into. The enemy can use drugs, alcohol, even medications to make you think you're so cool; everyone loves you when you're drunk. You think you're so much fun and that high feels amazing. Drinking, drugging and dealing may rake in a lot of money, and there may be some that will be impressed with it, or with your fast car, jewelry, clothes, and the most recent electronics – but at what cost?

Living a life of addictions will ruin you. You can reach a point where you won't remember how you lost relationships, family, business, money and the people who really loved you.

Make no mistake; he is not a mythical image with horns and a pitch fork. He is an evil spirit, and a hateful force here on earth. He's cunning and will provoke you to believe his lies while creating separation between you and your loved one. He will riddle you with fear or keep you addicted. He'll kill you if you let him. But the enemy knows the power and the authority that the name of Jesus holds. When you need Jesus to help you, call out His name and He will fight the demons for you. The devil trembles at His name, so call it out loud!

∞

Mathew 8:29

And behold, they cried out, saying, "What do we have
to do with You, Son of God? Have You come here to torment us
before the time?"

∞

Why would you continue to allow Satan to take control of your life, when God gave you a spirit of power, love and self-discipline? God gave you the authority to trample on demons and the power and self-control to stomp it out and win the bat-tle. It's up to you to use what God gave you and change your life; victory can be yours over every plot the enemy throws at you!God won't override your free will, but He wants you to ask for His help. He is there; waiting. If you feel like you're down to your last penny; you feel like a loser; or there's no hope for you, please understand and remember that nothing you've done can separate you from His love, except you. It's your choice to fol-low Satan's plot or to defeat him and claim victory and freedom with God.

When times seem so bad and life feels like it's not worth living – that's exactly where the enemy wants to get you; he's the feeder of lies. "Just do it once more; rob someone again; one more drug; another drink won't hurt." The feeder of lies will make you feel as if you can't change or that you are falsely in control. You know that something is missing in your life, things are wrong, but deep down you can feel that you can change things; that you can truly regain control – that's God! When you feel the truth pressing on you to make things right– trust that He's in there. With God nothing is impossible. He can raise you up and deliver you from any circumstance; no matter how you got there. God's plan is not to harm or judge you; His plan is to give you hope and a purpose. He wants you to have a life of abundance. Growing up, it was all around us. You had to decide which way you wanted to go.

We reminisced a while longer with the two ladies on the porch. I was amazed and excited that they knew many of the people I had grown up with. They were able to fill in years of who moved where; who went off to school or the military; who married who; who died and which ones got in trouble, and which ones succeeded. I thanked them, and we moved on to re-trace what I came to remember.

CHAPTER 5
DYSFUNCTION JUNCTION

Because you come from a dysfunctional family
doesn't mean you're destined for a dysfunctional life.

The old sewing factory was still on the corner; the windows were now covered in rusted wire mesh, and the steel doors pulled down and padlocked. It was once a very busy sewing center with rows of machines and needles bobbing up and down. The doors were almost always open, and the block smelled of fresh linen.

"Em, we used to play this game, 'Johnny-on-the Pony.' One person would put his head against the brick wall of the factory and bend at the waist, the next person put their arms around the first person's waist, and we continued to make a chain of people. The last person would get a running jump, leap on all our backs and get as close to the wall as he could. I guess it was kinda rough, but it was fun!" I laughed at how funny that sounded.

"Umm...yeah" Em smirked and smiled. "Real bright — that explains a few things."

In the summer we were always on bikes, up and down the blocks, under the train, and flying down the streets; sometimes falling, getting scraped, getting hurt — we were from the Bronx, it's the way we grew up — we were tough. We made up dances, put on plays in someone's garage. If you had a pool, you were the family every kid wanted to be friends with; otherwise we had fire hydrants or parents that took us to a nearby pool. We didn't have much, but the families on our block were intertwined like the climbing rose on the rail, thorns and all.

Despite the normalcy of growing up in a close-knit neighborhood where most mothers were inside cooking, and fathers came home from work in time for dinner, our family was different. The pungent and inviting smell of garlic and onions being sautéed in butter and olive oil with Italian sausage and peppers drifted out of every window, except ours.

My dad worked at night as an electrician, part-time as a bricklayer, and slept during the day. I remember helping him mix concrete. One of his tricks was to put Ivory powder, laundry detergent in it to keep it from drying too soon; it would also help to smooth it out while you were laying the bricks. But, he wasn't home to do normal family things; he didn't whistle for us to come in at night. He was the dad who was at the bar every night. Though I was only about 7-years old, my mother usually sent my brother and me to get him from the bar around the corner.

Taking a left at the sewing factory, we decided to walk around the entire block. The butcher shop was gone; in its place was a store selling curtains and things for the home. The raised train tracks ran down the center and the length of the street, connecting the Bronx to the subways of the city. The number of people had increased and diversified since the days that I had lived here. But, it still had the buzz of people rushing to get errands done, trucks delivering meat from Hunts Point, beautiful fruit and vegetable stands that enticed you to buy red plum to-

-matoes, green grapes, and gorgeous rainbows of flowers.

Back in the day, the people on the avenue all knew each other. We shopped at the small grocer, and we knew the local store owners. I loved going with my mother to pay bills, and the car insurance. The people in the office always made me feel so special. I'd give them a hug and they'd asked me how many boyfriends I had – and I remember my answer was 35! Donny Osmond, David Cassidy, Davy Jones, a bunch of boys in my class and my dad.

We turned at the next corner and passed the storefront where the bar once stood; a KFC, "Kennedy Fried Chicken & Pizza," had taken its place, but in my mind, the bar was still there.

"Em, my dad was a handsome man, very well liked and always had a story to tell from the barstool. He would buy himself more time by giving us quarters to play pool, which made us even later getting home. The three of us would stumble home most nights, listening to his stories. 'Come here pal,' he'd say. 'Always remember to treat other people the way you want to be treated; love God with all your heart and soul.' He truly meant it Em. No matter how mixed up his stories would get, the moral was always the same: If you could rely on one person in your life, you were fortunate."

There was never any doubt that my father loved us all. As a family, we prayed for him; as kids we prayed for him; his mother prayed for him.

∞

Mathew 18:19, NASB

"...if two of you agree on earth about anything that
they may ask, it shall be done for them by My Father
who is in heaven."

∞

My mother prayed for him, but she was a warrior! She didn't just leave it there! She took it to church and they prayed together as a congregation, they interceded for so many years. Despite his alcoholism, he went to work every day and supported us the best that he could.

"You know, my parents, and my friend's parents were the same way Jackie. My dad was in the Air Force, and as a security police officer in Denver, he often slept during the day and worked nights. As kids, we stayed outside until we got called in for dinner, or until it was practically time for bed. I don't know if it was the stress of the hours they worked, or if they found themselves as parents too young, but there were a lot of dads in my neighborhood that drank too much. They weren't all alcoholics, but most of my friend's dads, mine included, weren't quite as nice as your dad when they were drinking. Some may have been fun initially, but then something clicked in them, and they'd turn that corner and become nasty or mean. One wrong look and that blue nylon, military belt would come off and lash across your thigh. There was a lot of abuse in my neighborhood, and often every-one looked the other way. Some of the housing units were townhouse style. I used to hear our next-door neighbor, a tall strong guy, come home drunk, get into an argument and beat his barely 5-foot-tall wife. The yelling and hitting sounds and her crying for him to stop traumatized me. She wouldn't leave the house for days, but when she finally did, she went out with sunglasses and a scarf around her neck to cover the bruises. My dad talked to him a few times and finally threatened to turn him in or come over and physically put him in his place. I hated that guy and still remember his face and her cries. So many things come with alcoholism. Child abuse, domestic violence – hitting the ones that you love, then not remembering the next day."

"That breaks my heart Em. My father never raised his hand to us, he wasn't mean, and he did get sober. He used to fill in large segments of his life with his version of what he thought happened during those years. Dad sponsored a young man named Eddie through the AA meetings and took him under his wing. Eddie's been sober for many years now and remains great friends with my dad. They would go on fishing trips, and when they returned my father would tell us how breathtaking the views were. Eddie would tell us how Dad pointed out the lakes where he used to pitch a tent for us kids, and how he used to pack up our camping equipment in our station wagon the night before and get us ready. He talked about how he taught us to fish, then filet our catch that night and cook it over the campfire for our dinner."

I would feel my eyebrow lifting and my head start to lean to one side with a comical look, because that NEVER happened!

"Em, these things never happened! My mother wouldn't let him take us anywhere! The one time he took us to a Yankee's game, he almost lost us."

Being the eccentric character that he was, he exaggerated stories of the things he did with us; things that just never ever happened. Personally, I always got a kick out of it. I think in his heart, he wished that it happened or maybe he really does think it happened. My sister on the other hand, had very little patience and was less amused by his tales. She would just shake her head and say, "Crazy old man that never happened." My mom didn't find it very amusing either. She didn't have it easy prior to his sobriety; she shouldered the responsibilities that he couldn't. Though she had to figure things out on her own, she often gravitated toward her sister, Kay, who lived across the street.

Dad believed in his heart that he was being a good father, and to the best of his abilities, he was; but, Aunt Kay continuously divided them. My mother cared less about cleaning and cooking, and more about spending time with us. Since my father worked at night and needed to sleep during the day, she became creative about keeping us busy. On rainy days, she'd turn the table upside down, put a sheet over it, and we would huddle underneath it with a flashlight as she told us stories. In the summer, she volunteered at the local pool giving lessons;

we became excellent swimmers early in life. We were little guys diving off the board and swimming in the deep end.

In the fall, she'd let us jump into piles of leaves, skip rocks on the water, and roll down grassy hills. My mom loved the outdoors. Even in the thick of winter, she'd pack sandwiches, wrap them in tin foil, and put them back neatly into the plastic wonder bread bag; pack a thermos of hot chocolate and take us to the park to ice skate.

She was a good woman who taught us well and reasoned with us. She was a disciplinarian and didn't let us fight with one another – although we did when she wasn't around. But she wanted us to love each other and taught us that blood was thicker than water.

Dad made sure we knew how to do things and how to fix things in and around the house; my mother encouraged us to be independent, and we learned to fend for ourselves at an early age. If there wasn't a dinner, you learned how to make it. If your clothes needed to be washed or ironed, you did it yourself. We didn't always have a washer and dryer, so we would often pull our clothes in a little wagon, sometimes on a sled, to the laundromat. If you didn't do it, it didn't get done. As dysfunctional as we were, there was a lot of love in our family. My parents didn't cater to us, but they treated us well.

"Em, to say that my parent's lives were hard is probably quite an understatement. My mother was born in Brooklyn, one of the youngest of eight children. She never really knew her father; he was injured in the Navy and institutionalized, leaving her mother to raise all the children alone. Eventually it proved to be too much for one person, they were very poor, and my grandmother couldn't provide for all of them. At some point, she had no choice and placed them in a Catholic orphanage for several years. Sadly, my mother's younger brother and two little sisters were lost in the process and were never seen again."

"That's so sad Jackie. How many years were they there?"

"I don't really know. My mother didn't like to talk about it; it broke and strengthened her at the same time. The orphanages back then were very different than today's children's homes. Children were really given away to a place where they weren't treated well, and the adoption process wasn't sophisticated. The nuns were strict, she mentioned once that they made kids crawl on raw rice as punishment. They weren't allowed to have any contact with their mother and had no hope of any way out. At that young age, I can't imagine how frightened she must have been knowing that her family was gone. Just gone. Wondering what was going to happen to her? Will she be taken away by strangers or live there forever? Would her mother ever come for her? She and her sister Kay clung to each other and made a pact to never be separated. Their bond to stay together was so strong, that in later years it divided my family."

"You know, back then, orphanages weren't just for home

-less, or parentless kids; often mentally or physically challenged children were left there and institutionalized. Have you ever driven by the orphanage?"

"No, she never said where it was, just that it was in Brooklyn. Can you imagine being that close to home as a child but not able to go back? It breaks my heart thinking about what she must have endured."

"We have to check it out Jackie."

"How? She never said the name."

"Google it! How many can there be in Brooklyn? Didn't you say your grandmother lived off Knickerbocker Ave.?"

"Yea, I think it was Knickerbocker and Maple."

"Love the internet! Look! It says that the Angel Guardian Home was a Catholic orphanage in the Park Slope area of Brooklyn, on 12th Avenue and 64th Street. Established in 1899 by the Sisters of Mercy as an extension of the Convent of Mercy, at 237 Willoughby Avenue. They've been taking in orphans since 1863. This must be it Jackie. Both were about 25 to 30 minutes from your grandmother's home on Knicker-bocker Avenue. They have a Facebook page!"

"Em, I never even thought of trying to find it – that's gotta be it. My mother never wanted to talk about it, and I respected her wishes."

"Their site says that they closed their doors last year."

"You know Em, while there are sad and even cruel com-ments about orphanages, at least my mother and her brothers

Angel Guardian Home, Brooklyn, NY

and sisters had a place to go rather than exist homeless or on the streets."

"We're going Jackie. We can't just look at it on-line."

"Okay Sherlock, but let's get through the Bronx first."

At some point, my grandmother was able to get five of the children back. My mother was always very sensitive and protective of her mother, especially when people criticized her for giving up her children. Through it all, she believed that her mother loved her, and she tried to understand that they were so poor that there just wasn't any other choice.

When I was in kindergarten, her mother got stomach cancer and moved in with us. She and I used to sit in the window in the kitchen and make up stories about the train that always passed by the apartment. We'd say, "Here comes Philip the train!" My mom really loved her a lot. We'd take her out with us while my dad slept. We'd bring a big lawn chair and blankets and set her up as comfortably as we could, so she could watch us play in the park or skate on the ice. She died when I was about 6-years old; it completely devastated my mother. I remember watching her cry and unable to truly console her.

I must have been about 8-years old when my mother and Aunt Kay went to visit their father. It was the first time that they were really meeting him. He didn't know his children or his grandchildren; I don't really remember where it was. We weren't allowed to say anything about my grandmother's pass-

-ing, for fear he would go crazy. Though my mother never knew her father, she believed that her parents loved each other, and that it was the tragedy that had separated them.

Her oldest sister, Myrtle, married the man that started Otis elevators. They weren't really close, and I didn't meet my cousins till I was in my late 20's. They told me similar stories about their mom, and how she had developed problems because of the childhood they had endured. Charlotte was the next in line, then Kay, Wally her brother and then my mother. The youngest were the twins and one other child; the three that were lost while in the orphanage. Wally passed very young in his 20's from a brain aneurism. All the sisters have now passed as well.

Growing up, Aunt Kay and Aunt Charlotte lived in our neighborhood and stayed very close, but in an almost toxic way. My mother's faith carried her through the hardest times. Sadly, her hardest times had not even come yet. My dad grew up in Brooklyn and went into the Army at a very young age. He loved this country and served honorably. His parents divorced in a time when that wasn't acceptable, and his mother continued to live in Brooklyn. Every holiday he and I would drive out to pick her up; I always looked forward to the ride and seeing her.

"Em, he drove sooooo...slow; music blaring to Chicago, singing 'Does anybody know what time it is? Does anybody really care?' We eventually got to the little brownstone, singing and laughing."

My grandmother's house on Willoughby Avenue had a small tree in front with a low black iron fence that protected the flowers blooming around it. Inside, a beautiful staircase graced her hallway and her home always smelled like olive oil. Her hair was always done up nicely in a bun from the beauty salon. Unlike my mother who wasn't into wearing make-up, doing her hair or wearing fancy clothes, my grandmother was always so well put together. She was always ready to go with bags of groceries of whatever she needed to make for meals at our house. Gravy and meatballs, sausage and peppers, stuffed artichokes, and my favorite, stuffed shells! The house always smelled so good when she was there. Life somehow felt a little more normal with her around.

St. Anthony's Parish, Bronx, NY

CHAPTER 6
SAINT ANTHONY'S

"The wind blows wherever it wants. Just as you can hear the wind but can't tell where it comes from or where it is going, so you can't explain how people are born of the Spirit." John 3:8, NLT

Every Sunday, I walked up five blocks to St. Anthony's Parish; usually by myself and left my mother and everyone still sleeping. One of my first memories of walking to mass alone, was on one of the coldest days of winter. The snow was higher than I was tall. I remember taking in the sermon and being so in love with Jesus. The nine o'clock children's mass was done well, and I really soaked up the gospel.

"I spent my life going to church - alone most of the time."

"   "Wait, 5-years old and you got up, dressed yourself, and walked to church?"

"I loved it Em. I preferred not to be distracted and wanted to focus on the message. I'm sure I was quite the picture with my white fake rabbit fur coat and matching fur hat!"

"I can just see you pulling yourself together, very grown up, tiptoeing to shut the door behind you quietly and marching up the street with full determination and purpose."

"That was me! Walking home from church one morning, I had my jacket wrapped tight and my matching hat on. It was freezing cold and the wind took my hat; it blended with the snow and was gone before I knew it. I never found it, but I remembered calling out to Jesus for help; something I would do for the rest of my life."

"But, you never got your hat back. Didn't that confuse you that Jesus didn't help you?"

"You don't always get what you want Em, that's how life is. You can't see the air, but when the wind blows, you can feel it – that's kind of how Jesus is – He's real, you can't see Him, but you can feel His presence. As a child I felt Him and just trusted that He was always with me."

I've felt His presence several times throughout my life in different ways. A few years ago, on a Memorial Day weekend, I fell asleep comfortably for the night. The sheer white curtains billowed softly with the beginnings of a summer breeze and I drifted off into a dream. In the dream, my sister was lying in bed with me, but the comforter was missing. It was as if she knew that I was going to ask her where it was, and almost like reading her mind I could tell she didn't want to answer the question, but I asked her anyway. "Col, do you know what happened to the comforter?" She hesitated, then spoke, "Yes I do. I'm sorry, I didn't want to tell you this, but I spilled Pepsi on it; it's folded in the corner of the room. I'll pay you $150, it's ruined." I told her, "You're my sister, you don't have to pay me anything."

She fell asleep as I lay thinking and asked God why. Why God, is it so hard here? Why is it so hard for people to tell the truth and forgive? From the open window I started to see an amusement park, which would normally be a concrete parking lot for residents. A children's helicopter ride was going around. Suddenly the roof of my apartment began lifting off and I was looking up at a perfect blue sky. I couldn't help but notice a beautiful fluffy cloud on this gorgeous summer day.

My eyes stared up at the cloud, as the summer breeze gently blew it down to what should have been the parking lot, but instead it became a sandy tropical beach. My eyes were focused on the cloud as it settled upon the ocean, and as the waves rolled to the shore, Jesus Christ appeared out of the cloud and walked out of the water and onto the shore. I was now standing on the beach, watching Him walk out, completely dry. In awe and pure amazement, meeting Jesus was never something I expected to do now; only at the end of my life. I wondered what I would do at that time, thinking that I would drop to my knees in humility; but in the dream without any hesitation, I walked directly over to Him and He hugged me. It was the most familiar peaceful hug I've ever experienced. You know when you hold your child for the first time and it's your skin, and your breath that made him yours; I was His. He kissed me once on each cheek and held me in His embrace. He was the most beautiful person I had ever seen. My own mind could never create or imagine anyone more perfect. His skin was bronzed, with the most beautiful tan imaginable. His hair was shiny, medium brown, somewhat golden by the sun and smooth, and His muscle tone perfect, as though He lived on the healthiest diet plan possible. I could never be as perfectly fit and muscularly as He was, even if I ate healthy for the rest of my life. His smile was a brilliant white. No picture in any painting or movie can ever compare, and words can never live up to His beauty.

Our feet were in the waves of the water where the ocean met the shore, and I spoke to Him! Can you even grasp that I spoke to Him? I said, "Jesus it's You. I've waited my whole life to see You." I felt no sense of judgment even though I'm nowhere near deserving. Then I asked if I could go with Him now - I was ready! Something I would never have thought about in my waking life; I love my son and my family and friends. I had no intentions of leaving the earth that day, or any day soon. I thought I would live on for many, many, more years somewhere close to 102. I wanted to live a long life here for my son who would then be in his mid-70s. But standing there with Jesus, I was ready to leave and took His hands – I had been waiting my whole life for this moment – I was ready to go! My eyes didn't leave His and He said, "You will, but it's not your time yet. I need for you to stay here and continue teaching." I stood on the sand in the warmth of the day in agreement. My eyes opened, and I was awake in the present day of the next morning; though I had just met Jesus seconds ago. It was as real as the day I was living in. It was a life changing moment that affected me, how could it not? It was more than just a dream; He came to me and reinforced my calling. I can never – will never forget that.

When you walk into my home, the first thing you will see, is a large picture hanging over my desk. Most people see a white horse in motion, as if it were coming right out of the wall with a glow of a white light all around it. But if you look closer, you can see His white robe and the blood on the edges of His arms stretched out, but His face is not showing. The picture is in an ornate white plaster frame, with gold inlays. At the top of the frame, in gold paint, I wrote: *John 1: "In the begin-ning was the word and the word was with God and the word was God manifest into flesh."* Along the bottom in the same gold paint, I wrote: *Revelation 9: "...and behold a white horse; and He that sat upon him was called Faith-ful and True, and His name is called The Word of God."*

Jesus in all His Victory will be back for me and all His children. My picture doesn't display His face only the white horse and His hands stretched out; and I know that He is coming back for us, just like He said He would.

"Jesus is absolutely beautiful Em; His image is etched in my mind forever, something no picture can ever depict or replace. It's His spirit, His presence that fills every sense of our being, mind, body and soul that makes it impossible to draw or put into words. As a child, I had always felt His pres-ence. Growing up, we get lost in life and we have to pay clos-er attention to feel Him; but know that He is always there."

Since we had made the block and ended up back at the car, we decided to drive up to St. Anthony's. We waved goodbye to the ladies, still sitting on the porch. Pulling up to the church, though it was the one that I got married in, it wasn't the one I grew up in. The church and Catholic school that I attended as a child had been next door, and very different. Originally, it was a skinny white building with red doors, and a steeple that reached towards heaven. The stairs going up to the doors seemed like they went up forever. We only used the church on very special occasions, most of the year our services were held next door in our school auditorium. The auditorium was used for everything from a basketball court, to a volleyball court, to a stage for plays and choir events. But on Sunday, all the folding chairs came out in rows and the sermon took center stage. Weekly collections went towards the hope of one day building a new church. By the time I started 7th grade, it was built, and it was magnificent!

"Em, it's been years since I've been here, but it hasn't changed very much."

It was still a beautiful brick building with tall stained-glass windows. The simple, yet ornate, iron gate was padlocked. I ran my fingers over the gold metal letters that spelled out "Saint Anthony" and looked up at the cross that rose above the curved roofline.

"Isn't it a beautiful church Em? I spent so many years inside those walls, even got married at the altar. Now, it just seems wrong to be locked out."

"It is, I'm really disappointed that we can't go in. I would have loved to have seen the inside. We should come back one morning for mass."

"Em, they closed it down?"

"What? No, I thought it was just closed for the day. Why would it be closed, it looks brand new?"

"People don't go to church anymore. It's really a shame and incredibly sad. That's why books like this one and the courses I teach are even more important. We need fellowship. We've got to get back to God, Christ, and church."

Though it was closed now, it was still magnificent. Each brick had been laid by hand and the pride in craftsmanship and design was something to be very proud of. It just longed for people to come back into its doors. The church and the houses on the street hadn't changed very much. It's as if time stood still in some places, while it sped ahead in others.

"Can I help you?" A lady with silvery gray hair and tinted wire rimmed glasses was standing beside me. She couldn't have been more than five feet tall at best.

"Hi, I went to mass here growing up, and attended school next door." I replied. "Monsignor Guido and Father Molazzio led mass when I was a little girl."

"Oh, Monsignor has been gone a long time dear; and the school next door was renovated several years ago." She replied. "I live across the street; been there for over 40 years."

I had walked by her house so many times and never met her. A statue of the Virgin Mary was in her yard, with pink and lavender azaleas beginning to bloom next to it. We spoke a bit longer and parted ways. I turned around to see my friend disappear around the corner and raced after her.

Catching up, breathless, I asked, "Where ya going?"

"I saw one of the nuns go around the back, and in that door," she whispered. "Why are we whispering? And why are you stalking nuns?"

"I don't know – but I think we should knock on the door and ask her if you can go into the church, just for a second."

The nun was kind and spoke to us a few minutes, but said she was only visiting and didn't have the key to let us in, and no one else was around that could either. Sadly, I thanked her, and we continued our quest. The next chapter of my life would take place in Yonkers.

My parent's home in Yonkers – though only twenty minutes away, it may as well have been another state.

CHAPTER 7
ALCOHOLISM

"Then they cried out to the Lord in their trouble, and he brought them out of their distress. He stilled the storm to a whisper; the waves of the sea were hushed. They were glad when it grew calm, and he guided them to their desired haven." Psalm 107:28-30, NIV

Though my father worked hard and never missed a day, there were lay-offs at the company. It hit him hard and he had to find another job. He started doing what he knew how to do best, drink and bartend. Our family moved to Yonkers when I was thirteen. I didn't want to leave my school and friends, so I stayed with my Aunt Kay in the Bronx. But, after a few months, I just couldn't deal with her anymore and moved to Yonkers with the rest of my family. Though it was only twenty minutes away, it may as well have been another state. It was very different from my world in the Bronx.

A new house, still a Catholic school, but no longer the close-knit neighborhood that I had grown up in; no longer the love I had found in my favorite familiar church pew. We lived on a busy, main road, so playing in the street was impossible. Call for a friend to come out? There weren't any. The kids traveled in clicks; girls more interested in boys; boys more interested in girls. Though the acceptance level was not the same, life moved along at a normal pace. My church in the Bronx was still very much in my heart; and my favorite song helped me keep God in my heart and steady my world:

46

We will work with each other;

We will walk hand in hand;

They will know we are Christians by our love, by our love;

We will work with each other;

We will walk side by side; And they will know we are

Christians by our love, by our love.

"That's the house on the right, Em; the one with the metal awning over the porch." We pulled up to the house where my father still lived. Though I grew up in it, and still spend time there with him, it had a different feel today. The memories that I hadn't thought about in a very long time, were running through my mind.

When I was about sixteen, I commuted from Yonkers back to Co-Op City in the Bronx to attend high school. After school, I worked in a furniture and appliance store, then after a long day, I went back home to Yonkers. Despite the commute and long work hours, I did quite well academically. But on the weekends and free time, it was party time! Eileen had become my best friend at work; we're still friends. We would meet up with others and go dancing, hang out at the beach, a pool party or concert. At the end of the night, we would stop at the Eagle's Nest, where my dad bartended.

"Whaddya want to drink?" He'd ask. It was usually amaretto and ginger ale. We would play Frogger and pinball; he'd come from behind the bar and take his turn. At the end of the night, he would lock up and we'd walk home together. Dad was usually wobbly by then and I would tell him that he had to stop drinking. We'd get home and he'd start playing music and we'd sing together and dance. His favorite was the airplane dance

47

his hands out to the sides and in the air. Mom would come down the stairs and ask what we were up to; my dad was always loving and would just continue singing and dancing.

There were a lot of crazy moments in our house. When the phone rang, of course I always thought it was for me. So, I'd run out of my bedroom, down the stairs, jump the last four steps, hold on to the top of the bannister, spin around it and make a dash to the kitchen so I could answer the phone first! Somehow, despite my acrobatic abilities, he'd usually get to it before me. "You kill 'em, we chill 'em," he'd answer, as I tried to pull the phone from his hands and explain that it was just my dad.

"Em, there were times when friends were over, and he would walk by with just a towel around his waist. But they had parents who were alcoholics too; so, it was just sort of the way things were."

"Ha! I know. My friend's dad was notorious for that. But he would come outside in his tighty whities, scratching his belly, no t-shirt and call for her to come in. She was mortified."

For years I prayed that my father would be able to stop drinking. His mother prayed her whole life for him; my mother, the twins, my aunts and everyone in church prayed for him. It wasn't until a few years later, that my dad's alcoholism finally took a toll on his mental well-being.

∞

Habakkuk: 2-3, NASB
"For the vision is yet for the appointed time; it hastens toward the goal, and it will not fail. Though it tarries, wait for it; for it will certainly come..."

∞

At forty-five, his alcoholism was in full bloom. The shakes were terrible, and he began to experience DTs, hallucinations, and was afraid of things in life. He wanted to be confined and asked my mom and brother to just lock him in his room, so he couldn't get to any alcohol. We knew that wasn't the way to treat an alcoholic, the withdrawals had to be monitored. He had finally hit rock bottom and asked for help. Thank God he asked for help. We had no choice but to have him admitted to a rehab center to dry out.

Westchester Hospital was able to admit him, but since he had been in the Army, we were able to get him transferred to the Veterans Hospital in Montrose. I think it's a great method that alcoholics go away for the first three months to dry out and get counseling. Although alcoholism can be genetic, there are often underlying reasons and issues that cause people to drink. Without identifying and getting to the root of those problems, even if the person is dry, the problems persist, and relapses can occur. You can't heal or get past pain by masking things, it will only resurface. You must address the problems, seek counseling, gain understanding and acceptance. Jesus Christ and Alcoholics Anonymous (AA) meetings are really what it comes down to. He's the healer of all things and all bondages. You can't do it alone. But that's the wonderful thing about a relationship with Jesus - you're not alone!

There were so many facets to my dad's life. When I was growing up, he was a bricklayer, then he did security for a major bank. But when he got laid off, he began drinking more heavily, until he hit rock bottom. After rehab, he attended AA meetings and started driving a truck for a fish store to help someone out;

he earned a reputation as a Good Samaritan.

Through AA, he met Dennis, a doorman who helped him get into the Doorman's Union and eventually got him a job in New York City in a wealthy building on 79th Street. Dad was very charismatic and sociable with everyone. He got some great stock advice and started learning about the market and began investing a little at a time. Remaining strong minded, he never fell off the wagon, instead he began forming and leading AA Groups all around Yonkers and started sponsoring others. What was once his mess, became his message. God turned my father's alcoholism around for the good of others.

True to form, not really knowing how it happened, Dad ended up as the President of the Doorman's Union. After thirty years, he retired with great benefits. He loved that job, it fit his personality, social and outgoing. Guess we know where I get it from! He was really something. He would get up at 4:00 a.m. and exercise; do all his praying; get the newspaper; have his coffee; walk to the train and get to work early. He was a positive energy person, loved God, his family and loved his Yankees and the Jets!

While he was a doorman, he met a producer in his building that thought he would be good on The Peoples Court as an extra. Most people need agents and an interview. Not my Dad! Next thing you know he's being picked up in a limo! He would always crack me up and say "Jacquelyn, I don't know how this stuff happens. It's not easy being in such high demand!"

Walking by the filming of the movie Scorpion, he was asked to do a small part and called me to ask if I would put streaks in his hair; kind of salt and pepper, like George Clooney. But he didn't wait for me and had one of his friends dye his hair.

His friend had no idea how to do hair! It looked awful and had gone from naturally white to dull brown. The movie gig didn't work out, the filming moved to Cali, but that didn't faze him; he was already off on another adventure!

I'm thankful that my dad was strong enough to admit that he was an alcoholic and went into rehab; because of it, he has been sober for over 35 years without ever slipping. A magnificent counselor and sponsor, to this day he holds meetings to help others. He's gone from a man that I've always loved as a child, to a man that has become my hero, my rock, and always full of unconditional love. To change your life, you've got to be honest and accountable, and he doesn't take any "B.S." He will tell you like it is. Dad was a character, but when it came to AA, it was no nonsense.

There is power in prayer to change what looks like the impossible. While it may take a person reaching the point of wanting and admitting that they need help and change, God's grace works behind the scenes when you ask. He will help you locate places, hospitals, ways and tools; and send people to work beside you. Keep praying and trusting in God, He is mighty and able to deliver you and your loved ones. Oh, my dad is still crazy in other ways! But he honestly is a real miracle and a success in his own right. I don't take that for granted and am incredibly proud of him.

CHAPTER 8
SPIRIT OF RELIGION "PHARISEE"

*"Do not judge, or you too will be judged. For in the same
way you judge others, you will be judged, and with the
measure you use, it will be measured to you."*
Matthew 7:1-2, NIV

Though my father had been the sole provider for many
years, unfortunately, after being away in rehab, he no longer
had an income. Mom had to pick up where he left off. She
waitressed; was a caretaker for a sick person; had several different part time positions and did her best to keep the family
afloat. When Dad returned home, he got right out there and
found a secure job and took the time to catch up and rebuild.
When an alcoholic sobers up, he begins to see all the flaws or
problems that he hadn't seen before. Now that he was sober,
he was energized and ready to start his life all over. Which was
great for him; unfortunately, by the time he obtained sobriety, it
had taken a toll on my mother. She had always been the sound
parent that raised us, but, the tide had turned. She began to
sleep a lot and the house was not taken care of. I finally
realized that she had slipped into depression.

After getting out of the orphanage, Mom and Aunt Kay
had made the pact to never let anything separate them again.
Even as adults, they remained joined at the hip. Kay was a very
domineering, demanding person that never got married or had
children; and really ordered my mother around and treated her

like a child. She knew how to manipulate and stomp out of the house, knowing that my mother's loyalty would cause her to chase after her. Mom's depression only deepened the bond with her sister, and she became first in my mother's life; first over my father; first over her children. My mother loved us, and we loved her, so we tried to understand and make exceptions for their toxic relationship, but the divide between my parents became not only emotional, but physical.

The house in Yonkers had four floors, my mother ended up living upstairs on the fourth floor, and my father slept in his own bedroom on the third floor. My father's mother moved from Brooklyn to our house, into an apartment on the ground level. Though it was attached, it had its own entrance and was separated from where the rest of the family lived. She never felt comfortable about coming in, unless she was invited for Christmas or something, so she rarely came upstairs; honestly, my mother didn't want her to come up. She felt that my grandmother had never accepted her into their family and thought that she talked badly about her to others. That really bothered me, I loved my grandmother and doubted that she had ever bad mouthed my mom. I think it was how my mother felt and my aunt made sure to go along with it, and most likely instigated it.

My grandmother would sit outside on the sidewalk in her folding chair while my mother and her sister sat on the balcony above her. They would have ice cream or a barbeque in the backyard, but never once invited her. It wasn't right to treat her that way. My grandmother would make gravy, and my father would go downstairs and have dinner with her. Her home was always neat; I just enjoyed her so much.

"Where did your aunt live? Didn't she live in the Bronx?"

"It turned out that the house next door had an apartment like the one my grandmother had in our house, and my aunt ended up moving into it. She really wanted the apartment that my grandmother had and was just waiting for my grandmother to die so she could get it."

Though my father was respectful of their relationship, he didn't want my aunt to move into the house. She really didn't have to since she lived next door and had no problem just walking in the door, disrupting everyone's lives; and my mother allowed it.

I would try to do nice things for my family. I'd bring everything for a barbeque, the chicken, the meat, bread, sides and salads, you name it. They would sit in the yard while I washed their cars; my father reading the paper. Once he mentioned that he'd like to see the Austin Powers movie and Kay nagged him and carried on. "How can you be a Christian and see that movie." I told her to just leave him alone! My mother chimed in and told me not to stick up for my father, but I argued back, "Why can't he see a movie, if he wants to see a movie?" Next thing you know, my aunts leaving and my mother's following her out. Over her shoulder while chasing after my aunt, my mother said, "You're really not right Jackie, not right." We were all divided once again! But Dad and I continued to hang out together in the yard, listening to the Yankee game, enjoying our barbeque and reading the Sunday paper. We loved my mother enough to put up with my aunt, but we refused to allow Aunt Kay's "spirit of religion" to control us. I cringe when people think I'm religious. Sometimes religion becomes more about the 'laws,' that we miss the heart. By focusing on repeating what's on the pages of books, saying it hard on Sunday then returning to normal life on Monday, we can miss the whole thing. Religious denominations often use their "laws" to rule lives. Rather than showing the heart of Jesus, they become wrapped up in the "legality" and are more concerned with how people in church dress, their behavior, how they eat, if they curse, or smoke. They turn people off with their judgments and do more harm than good. The Bible describes this as the Spirit of Pharisee - someone who is in the church but dominated by religious laws. That's the danger in religion. The man-made "laws" can distance us from a relationship with God.

My aunt was toxic, controlling and manipulative. She was toxic to my parent's relationship; she was toxic to my mother. Aunt Kay could be sweet, but it was short lived and fake. She ate at our house almost every day then hounded us to say grace as she finished loading up her plate! We would all hold hands with our empty plates, and say the prayer. Before the last word barely out of our mouths, she would dive in. Praying before a meal is something that should come from the heart and being truly thankful for what you have, for her it was more of a formality. The same way that she went to church every single weekend and prayed the loudest to impress others to show that she was holy and militant about saying the prayer. It was almost like a rehearsed chant, with no true meaning in it – just something memorized to be repeated.

"Jackie, I have to wonder if it doesn't have something to do with her childhood and living in the orphanage. Maybe that's where religion became a formality for her; a regiment forced to be followed, rather than a saving grace and way of hope."

"Maybe. But I think it's just who she was. She believed in God, but sadly didn't really develop a relationship with Jesus. She didn't get to know who He is, who God really is."

"It's interesting though, that your mom, despite what she must have gone through, came away from there with love still in her heart."

"My mom developed a strong relationship with the Lord and through everything in her life, she still loved; she loved us, her husband, her mother, and her brothers and sisters."

The town of Dobbs Ferry has a beautiful park on the Hudson River. In the summer, they had concerts at sunset. It was meant to be enjoyed by all and a reminder to be thankful for the day and the people around you. My mom loved it; but Aunt Kay was always critical of everyone and everything. "Those people are talking too loudly; that group is smoking; they're cursing... it's too hot...there's too much traffic getting here, too much traffic going home." There was always something; always a complaint.

During my sister's wedding, she complained that the air conditioning was too cold, the DJ too loud, and pouted, and carried on, threatening to leave if things weren't adjusted to her way; anything to manipulate my mother to chase after her and prevent her from enjoying my sister's wedding. Everyone else was having a wonderful time and of course my father and I were singing and dancing up a storm! I'd like to say it was because of their childhood; but honestly, it's the person that we are on the inside that matters. My mom, despite what she was exposed to growing up, was still a loving person; my Aunt just wasn't.

Aunt Kay didn't really have any true friends, she would try to manipulate them, and they were smart enough not to tolerate it. She couldn't hold a job and always had an excuse for everything: she was too smart, too short, not domesticated enough. She went on Section 8 and took advantage of the system. She just wasn't fun to be around. People with the Spirit of Religion, also referred to as the Spirit of Pharisee, hide their own sins secretly while casting judgment on others. Some behaviors and sins are easier to notice, while others are kept as secrets, like lying, treating the ones you "love" poorly behind closed doors, gossip, manipulation, violence.

I have a very close friend who gave his life to the Lord and recently admitted that he was gay. He doesn't struggle with his decision to come out, or that he's a Christian, but he still struggles with the assessment others make about him. How can you be gay and a Christian? When he goes to church he instantly feels judged. It's broken his faith and has separated him from God. I always tell him to thank God for his salvation and to not lose his relationship with the Lord because of people that hide behind religious "laws."

It's one reason why some people won't go to temples and churches; they feel they will be judged when they walk in. That's not the way anyone who enters should feel or be treated. Jesus did not come here to die for a few, He came here because we are all sinners. It is because of His grace that those who accept Him are saved. It's a gift to us if we receive it. Jesus wants our relationship not a religion. We are all works in progress, and if we listen, He will guide the way to deliverance; but listening and applying His guidance is up to us. Our responsibility as Christians is to guide with love. His fruits of love, peace, joy, kindness, goodness, patience, self-control, and gentleness are what we're supposed to reap and then sow into others. We should be a beacon of light shining bright so that more will see His love in us and want it too.

When my Aunt Kay passed away in 2005 from brain cancer, of course my mother missed her terribly, but she finally realized, or at least allowed herself to accept a lot of the damage that was caused by her sister and their relationship. My aunt didn't like this life, so my mom felt some peace knowing that my aunt was now with Jesus and their mother. Mom finally had more time for us and in some ways, it helped us to reconcile the past.

The sad thing about Kay's passing, was that she was scared. For all the years that she had gone to church, she was afraid to die. In part, because she never really had the relationship with Jesus that she should have had. I don't think she knew that she had been loved all along. The laws kept her trapped when she could have been free to enjoy her days like everyone else. The only people at her funeral were immediate family members, a couple of people from the old neighborhood, and a few from church that felt obligated. But, nothing personal, nothing intimate. What memories of her were left behind? Sadly, not many good ones.

Ask yourself how you want your life to be remembered or defined when you're gone. Will you leave a legacy? People in relationships? Did you accomplish anything? Were you the glue of the family, or were you arrogant and prideful? Did you love? Were you loved? Though my aunt went to church every day, she never had the relationship she was meant to have with Christ, because of that she never really had true joy. She did have salvation, because she accepted Jesus was her Lord and Savior, but she never built on that relationship, and she never got to the heart of what it was meant to be. There's no reason why she couldn't have had a good life, instead she became more concerned about what everyone else was doing; and perhaps held so tightly to things in her past that she couldn't be in the present.

Jesus didn't come here to control people. Right before He left this earth, He told us to "Love one another, the way that I have loved you." If we could show the love of Jesus through our words and actions, others would be more inclined to want to be part of His kingdom. When we judge and police others, it gives God and Jesus a bad name; man-made interpretations of religion divide us rather than unify us.

Remember that God is all about hearts, about love. God is love. He doesn't care who prays the loudest, what you drive, or what your house looks like. He cares about you – no one is insignificant – no matter where they live, what they do, who they think they are – who they wish they were. He doesn't care that someone didn't start believing in Him in the past, or that they questioned His existence. He only cares that they start where they are now.

CHAPTER 9
GUILT & CONSEQUENCES

"Then I acknowledged my sin to you and did not cover up my iniquity. I said, 'I will confess my transgressions to the LORD' and You forgave the guilt of my sin."
Psalm 32:5, NIV

In my teens, I learned how to deal with my home being divided. My sister was Switzerland – generally neutral. Since my father really wasn't a great role model in his drinking years, my brother aligned more with my mother and took her side on things. Though I tended to be more on my dad's side, I did love my mother, so I made concessions by being tolerant of my aunt's behavior - to a point. I enjoyed being social and had a lot of fun right from the start. I had friends on my block, friends around the corner, friends a few blocks over; to this day I like to be out, active, and visiting different friends all over the place. Growing up, I was a cheerleader, was on the basketball team, played second base on the softball team, in the dance club, and had a lot of passion, hobbies, and interests outside of the house, and I always loved to work.

At fifteen, I met Larry; he was twenty-one. My mother didn't realize our age difference, since he looked younger. With his "guidance," I grew up very quickly. Six-months after we started dating, wanting to be closer to me, he moved three houses down from my parents. I worked at a furniture store in the Bronx and went to high school, he often drove me back and forth. We dated till I was eighteen.

He was serious and wanted to get married, but I had started experiencing life outside of school and work; clubs, dancing, enjoying life – spreading my wings and allowing myself to fly. I knew I wasn't ready for marriage and that I needed to end the relationship.

A couple of weeks passed by in silence and on November 21st I met Joe while dancing with my friend Eileen, at the Left Bank, a punk rock club in Mt. Vernon. He reminded me of Lorenzo Lamas and drove a shiny white El Dorado with white leather seats – kind of like a pimp mobile now that I think about it. Punk Rock clubs were a rough scene with slam dancing. Joe saw someone slam into me and came over to see if I was okay. We started talking and he offered to take Eileen and me to a calmer club. We danced late into the morning to disco music, The Jackson 5 and Prince.

The sun was coming up and Saturday night had turned into Sunday morning. We dropped Eileen off, and I asked Joe to drive me to church – he did. It was an Italian mass and we sat through it together. After mass, he went home and told his mother that he met this girl with a cute squeaky voice - Joe didn't exactly have a great grasp of language! He said that I was a good girl, one that his mother would approve of.

About a month later, we had sex for the first time. It was New Year's Eve and we had left a party sometime after midnight. Driving around a blind bend in the road with a double yellow line, headlights came at us from both lanes, as two cars drag racing, barreled towards us at top speed.

"We couldn't get out of the way Em. BAM! Head on

collision. It was too late. The drivers were drunk. The El Dorado, a big car, saved us that night, but the lives lost in the other car somehow bonded us. Em, I don't think I ever really fell in love with Joe, but that tragedy and circumstances over the following months sealed our fate."

I went to a free clinic only to hear "you're pregnant." I don't remember what I did when I left; I don't remember anything else that was said. I just knew that I didn't want it to be true. My mother was a devout, very pro-life activist, with strong convictions; how would she take it? Joe wanted to keep the baby; I just didn't know how to afford or raise a child. I made the appointment for the abortion and went to the clinic without him. Joe was absent from everything responsible – something I learned more about as years went on.

I'd like to tell you that it was a cold, rainy and gray day that I went to the clinic. But I can't remember anything except feeling awful. At that age, I didn't ask any questions and was just set on getting it done. I remember just going through with the procedure – that's what it was - a procedure. I laid there with my eyes open, waiting to hear that it was over. My mind in a fog, I got off the table and went to Joe's apartment. Of course, everyone was there, his sister, her children and other family members. The abortion left me feeling sore and numb; we just told everyone that I had been at the dentist and had a toothache. We made a pact never to tell anyone; my mother never found out. At eighteen, I took the life of my unborn child; then intentionally covered it up. To me, it was the most horrible sin I could have ever committed.

Three days after the abortion, on my nineteenth birthday, Joe took me to The Charthouse in Dobbs Ferry, a beautiful restaurant on the river. He opened a small velvet box with a diamond engagement ring and asked me to marry him. Though my words said 'Yes,' my heart didn't. But, after the horrible car accident and what we had just gone through with the abortion, I guess I felt that I owed it to him. The guilt I carried from having the abortion, somehow made me feel that by marrying him, I could right a wrong. My parents didn't understand why we were getting married so soon. My mother wanted me to work and have a career, meet more people. My father thought I should travel and see the world; I was young and had my whole life ahead of me. I went through with it anyway and kept my secret.

Three months later, on a very hot, June day, in a white dress, white tux, white limo, we were married at St. Anthony's church. We said, "I do" and consummated a marriage that I would endure for all the wrong reasons. I still prayed, but felt shame, unforgiven, and trapped in my self-imposed bondage.

Marriage became my own self-created penance for the guilt of the abortion. The consequences of my choices prevented me from all the dreams I had for myself, and of those my parents had for me. Though I didn't realize it at the time, I had entered an abusive relationship and would over time accept all of Joe's cruelty and abuse, convinced that I somehow deserved it. When I contemplated divorce, I worried that I would once again disappoint God.

For years I continued to carry that shame and guilt, not

even my best friend knew. It wasn't until many years later that I discussed it with a friend at work who confessed to me that she had gone through an abortion as well.

After I got to really know the Holy Spirit in my late twenty's, I attended a day retreat with my mother, and during a workshop, the teacher spoke about abortion and losing a child. She said that you could name the child; that the spirit still existed, and that the soul had gone on to heaven. I had always felt that the baby would have been a girl; that day I gave her a name. Even though the child was never born, it still had a soul that was raised back to heaven and received eternal life.

There are still times that I think of that baby and how old she would have been today and what she would have been like. I hope that when I'm in heaven, I'll see her, tell her that I'm sorry and that I love her, and I hope that she will love me back.

"Em, I was truly sorry. Hiding that sin kept me stuck and anchored to shame for many years. What a horrible way to live."

We are all sinners. God sees and knows our sin even if we try to hide it. When we confess them to Him with sincere repentance, no matter how horrible that sin is, He will forgive us. I learned that if you're truly sorry, just tell Him, be free of it. No matter what you do, you're His child and He wants you to be in a relationship with Him; no matter what.

"Jackie, I fell in love when I was eighteen. We had a wonderful romance until I found out that he had cheated on me. I planned to leave him, but found out that I was pregnant. The birth control pills hadn't quite taken affect and I was faced with the same decision. I had just started my career.

I contemplated abortion, made my appointment and had a friend drive me to the clinic, but I couldn't go in. I went back to the dorm and cried and cut myself off from everyone. Shame consumed me, pregnant at 18. My 'friends' judged and ignored me and went on with their partying, giving me sideward glances of disgust; my supervisor was disappointed in me and said that he used to have high hopes for me and had expected more from me. I felt as if I had a huge label on my back as a bad person and that God was nowhere in the picture. My life was ruined – a child having a child – how was I going to do this?

I made another appointment for the abortion and was determined to keep it this time. I struggled with the guilt for two weeks, then three days before the procedure, running down the stairs to get to the phone, I tripped over a couple making out on the stairs and I fell down half a flight. In that moment I felt that the fall had killed my unborn child. That guilt overrode everything else that I had felt, and I made my way back to my room, crying and praying. I prayed for the life inside me to continue; I prayed for God to forgive me for getting pregnant; to forgive me for my intentions for the abortion. The next day I started cramping and throwing up and went to the ER. They couldn't find a heartbeat and determined that I had aborted the baby in the fall. They made the appointment for me to come back in a few days for the D&C if my body didn't abort it on its own. I was devastated and never prayed so hard in my life for forgiveness; it felt like God said "Okay, you don't want it – you don't deserve this child."

"God's not like that Em. He's not cruel."

"Wish I had known that back then. I was an emotional mess. My parents were ashamed and embarrassed."

My boyfriend had been reassigned across the country and was out of the picture. With no one to turn to, I had never felt so alone in my life. That's when I turned to God. I made every promise I could think of; I asked for forgiveness for everything I did or may have done in my life that He objected to; I prayed for days for Him to breathe life back into this child that I could no longer feel.

The night before the procedure, exhausted from the worry, the guilt, and the unfulfilled prayers, I attempted a final prayer to God; and as an amazing calm came over me, I "heard" in my mind "You are forgiven; rest now and know that your child is fine." The next morning, reluctantly, I went to the D&C appointment and insisted that they check me again. They ignored my repeated requests and started to prep me for the procedure. I refused and insisted that they check me one more time; they finally did to humor me, or maybe just to shut me up. Jackie the heartbeat was there! I jumped off that exam table so fast and bolted out of the room! Now I have my beautiful Nicole and cannot imagine what my life would have been without her. My point is that the guilt that you carried in your heart for the abortion, was forgiven a long time ago. We are only human, we are going to make mistakes or very wrong choices in this life. But, because He forgives and loves us, we can move on in this life."

"I know that now. I still feel the loss of my child, but when I truly repented God forgave me. I was so very sorry. God knew my heart and He knew that I would never do that again. While some convicting guilt is good and tells us that we did something very wrong, holding on to it for years, trying to right a wrong is also a sinful guilt. Knowing that God forgave me broke that bondage. I didn't need to continue paying the emotional price – it was done. He removed it."

If God forgave me, who was I, so much less than Him, to not forgive myself. I'm not saying abortion is right or justified; just that God forgives, no matter how great our sin is.

CHAPTER 10
ABUSE & CONTROL

"Do you think that I have come to give peace on earth? No, I tell you, but rather division. From now on in one house, there will be five divided, three against two, two against three. They will be divided, father against son, son against father, mother against daughter, daughter against mother, mother-in-law against daughter-in-law, daughter-in-law against mother-in-law." Luke 12: 51-53, NIV

Old world Italian families claim closeness, but problems and secrets run deep. Joe was managing the deli department of a large grocery store; I took two buses to work, did the grocery shopping, and tried to do everything right. That was our honeymoon.

Joe's father, Duke, was an alcoholic, and emotionally and physically abusive; though he did refrain from the abuse when I moved in, his alcoholism continued to rage. Because of Duke's bad credit, the one-bedroom apartment Joe and his parents lived in was under Joe's name. The deal was, that I'd move in there, and his parents would look for a new place, but the bedroom was theirs while they lived there.

We had a small working kitchen with a foyer like dining area, a living room that was divided, and our bed to one side. The telephone cord from the kitchen reached into the dining area, and my mother-in-law sat and talked on the phone for hours. Not exactly the best living conditions for a young, newly married couple that already had a lot of issues to sort through. I loved her, but it was suffocating, and we didn't have an ounce of privacy or quality time. Three years went by like that; she and Duke were in no hurry to move out. So much for the deal!

Duke was a tough guy; looked like Charles Bronson and would think nothing of hitting a brick wall with his fist and breaking his hand. He liked his Southern Comfort and carried it in a flask to Atlantic City or the Yonkers race track to bet on the horses. He would always say to his wife "Come on let's go! We'll see a show, you can sit on the beach!" But 90% of the time, it turned into a six-hour, round-trip ride and back the same day. No show, no beach, no money, but always full of stories of how high up he was winning before he lost it all and always with a new strategy of how he would win it back the next time.

One night, rolling dice at the craps table in Atlantic City, he suffered a heart attack. In a blizzard, with zero visibility for most of the ride, Joe and I drove through the night. By the time we got to the hospital, Duke had released himself and was already back in the casino with a drink, cigarettes, and a bet on the table. Joe didn't have anyone to model himself after; sadly, like so many men, he followed in his father's footsteps. He became a gambler and an extremely jealous and abusive person. Though Joe never physically hit me, the emotional abuse was just as damaging. That's the way he grew up, that's what he knew, and that's what he became.

"Did Duke try to get help?"

"No. Though my dad broke free of alcoholism, Duke never wanted to change."

There were many good things about Duke; when he won he was very generous. Deep down I think he really wanted to win, not just for himself, but for everyone else. He had plans that when he won big, he would make everyone financially comfortable and rich. There was never any consideration of changing; and he didn't.

Three years later, we finally managed to get into our own apartment, but my life was still controlled.

"Where did you move to?"

"We stayed in Yonkers. Come on, I'll show you."

We left my dad's house and drove to the first apartment Joe and I had shared. Storm clouds had formed in the distance and threatened to catch up with us. As we got closer to the apartment, the sky grew darker with the approaching storm, very appropriate and in line with my mood and those years of my life. By the time we pulled up to the building, the skies had opened up and the rain beat down on the car, and the day looked like night.

"Em, I had to dress covered up and frumpy. He constantly questioned my clothes. I lived in what felt like a potato sack – even then he would interrogate me! My shirts always had to be buttoned up to the top, always baggy, no bright colors; nothing that might gain any attention. At such a young age, even having a great body, I looked old, frumpy and ridiculous. He had such double standards. The girls he worked with wore shorts and feminine or form fitting things and that was okay. It was normal to be in shorts or short sleeve shirts in the summer, but I wasn't allowed to. I was 102 pounds and he'd say, "You're fat."

When he took pictures or videos of family gatherings, he would exclude me from them as if I weren't even present. Once we were driving to his sister's house and passed a bill-

-board of the male Calvin Klein underwear model. I made the mistake of looking at it and that was it! He accused me all day of staring at the crotch on the model. We could drive or be in the same room, and never speak – I didn't want to talk to him – we had nothing to discuss.

He had to approve of everything I wore and who I spoke to; He was critical of me, and every person I became friends with. He'd check the mileage on my car to see how far I went each day; take the spark plugs out to prevent me from leaving; and always questioned every move I made and everything I did. "How come you're home in 30 minutes to-day, but yesterday you were home in 20? What did you do? Where did you go? Who did you talk to? Did anyone bother you? Why did you brush your teeth to go to the dentist?" In-sinuating that I had something going on with the dentist. Any-thing, anyone, would just trigger his jealousy and insecurities.

If I made a comment about an area as we drove by, it turned into "When were you there? Why were you there? Who were you there with?" He would go into my purse and search for something incriminating. Once he opened a let-ter from a childhood friend – she said let's get together and catch up. He forbid me to go and made me disassociate my-self from her. If he met my friends from work, he would in-stantly not like this one or that one for unfounded reasons.

My friend Rosa, still my friend today, was having a bach-elorette party at a comedy club. She was such a good friend, and I was so sick of always making up excuses as to why I couldn't do things or go places. So, I decided that I was going to the party, the place was called Try Outs – comedians doing standup comedy. The sarcastic accusations started as soon as I walked in the door "Who are you going to try out?" I always felt like I was in a mafia drill, repeatedly being questioned to see if my answers would change. He was relentless, in his mind I was always guilty. After years of his abuse, I was finally able to go to a gym; a small, all woman's gym, and only with people he and his mother knew. She would show up randomly when I was in an aerobics class to "say hello." While I'm bouncing around in a class! I would have to stop and say "hello" or I'd hear about it when I got home! When I went to church he'd question who went; who did I sit with? Even if it was with my parents. I never really told them how bad it was.

He rarely came to things with my family; sometimes for a holiday but very begrudgingly, and he was always tired. He was still in his 20's, but always with an excuse. I was always fearful of someone mentioning anyone's name; a previous boyfriend that still lived on the same block; or a family friend; any male name and I would feel my blood drain. The control was horrible; there were a lot of good people that I met but, in his mind, every woman was basically a pig.

Once my mother whispered something to my aunt and he held that paranoid resentment against her for the rest of her life. He would compare his mother who called every single day, and came to the house constantly, with my mother, "she doesn't do this, and she doesn't do that."

I left him a few times; my mother would help me, but I always went back, hoping it would work out this time. It's hard to give up the things you worked for – furniture, apartment –

we moved again and hoped for a new start.

I know we should love one another the way that Jesus loves us. When I married and took a vow to love my husband, I showed him Jesus' love by example and stayed faithful to His teachings, but my husband remained verbally and emotionally abusive. Although, I knew that Jesus loved me no matter what Joe said to me; the problem was that Joe wasn't loving me; he wasn't learning from my example. Joe didn't love himself, how could he love me?

We get confused about that and try to love someone so much and believe that the other person will finally understand and give it back. I think that's what I tried to do for over ten years, questioning, going to church, praying and hoping things would get better – but it just continued; there was no end to it.

Our new home should have been a home full of love; a place for the two of us to finally get a fresh start. I thought our marital problems could be better worked out if we were on our own, yet his family still showed up constantly announced or un-announced; invited or not invited. When they weren't physically there, they were on the phone; and always right at dinner time, and of course he took the calls every time. My mother-in-law meddled in everything and manipulated situations to fit her mood. She always had a dig "Where is she now? How come she's later today than yesterday?" It just further fueled Joe's paranoia. Then she would switch to being on my side and convoluted the situation.

As his emotional abuse continued and escalated he add-ed financial abuse to his list of controls. I wasn't allowed to do anything or go anywhere, and he would give me just enough money to get to and from work. I had no money, no independ-

-ence; no freedom. I've always been a very hardworking woman, and have always had excellent work ethics, but, my paycheck was handed over to him the minute I got it, and he usually gambled it away as soon as it was cashed. He was such a gambler and when he did win, it wasn't shared with me. He would help his family here and there, but never anything to me – in his eyes, I was no good.   ∞

1 Corinthians: 10-13, NASB

No temptation has overtaken you but such as is common to man; and God is faithful, who will not allow you to be tempted beyond what you are able, but with the temptation will provide the way of escape also, that you may be able to endure it."

∞

"Financial abuse is a very real method of control Jackie. Bill did the same with me. After we got married, I had my second daughter and stayed home for three years. He insisted on "managing" the money. He constantly changed bank accounts and wouldn't put my name on them, claiming that it was to protect me from any of his business issues. He said not to worry about it, that he would give me what I needed. Wrapped up with taking care of my children and his sick mother, I was concerned, but had a lot of other things on my plate at that point. He was a talented builder, but a lousy businessman. Struggling financially, he began to drink more and became verbally and emotionally abusive. I knew I had to get myself and my girls out of it, but I didn't know how. We had money, but I didn't have access to it. I didn't have the means to rent a place, buy furniture, food, or clothes for them, and I didn't have family that was in the position to help. That was the main reason I stayed so long. I hated that my girls had to endure the emotional damage and be subjected to our fighting. Initially, he wasn't physically abusive, but eventually that changed. I remember thinking 'How the hell did I get to this point in my life? How did I let this happen? How do I get my girls and myself out of it?"

"You're not alone Em, it can happen subtly, and you don't even realize it until it's too far gone, or it can be abrupt and even violent. It's a powerful way of keeping someone trapped in an abusive relationship. He probably told you he was doing it out of love; to care for you and the family, and you had no reason not to trust or believe him. You expect that in a relationship, and especially in a marriage. It sounds like a classic case of financial abuse. How did you get out of it?"

"I told him that I wanted to go back to work, my youngest was old enough for daycare and it would help us financially. He was fine with it, but when I went back to work, as soon as I got off the train and into the car, I had to hand over my paycheck or face constant badgering and arguing. No direct deposit, he insisted on a paper check. To keep the peace, I did as he asked – he was relentless. I was commuting to the city and barely had enough to get there and back. I didn't have enough money to go to lunch with friends and always had to come up with an excuse. "I have a deadline, or boss needs something; or have to run an errand." The control continued, but I still couldn't leave. After a few months, I told him that the company had gone to an all direct deposit system and no longer did paper checks. I had just gotten a raise, so I opened an account without him knowing, and was able to split the money between his account and mine.

When I received my bonus, I told him that we didn't get one. It was a private firm and they didn't make enough to give bonuses that year. It was actually $10,000 and it went right into my other account as I started making my plans to move."

"Were you able to get out then?"

"No, it took a while, I didn't know it, but since he had my social security number, he had opened up a business in my name, owed several years of sales tax and had built up debt. My credit was shot. After a few months, I had enough saved, a reference letter from my employer; and put down one month's rent and two months security and I had a home to move my girls to."

"Em, I had never heard of financial abuse until recently. I knew I was living it, but not that so many others were as well. As with all forms of abuse, it doesn't matter how educated you are or what your social or ethnic group is, abuse is abuse and it doesn't discriminate. I think the main thing to understand and remember is that there is always a way out. There are organizations, churches, information on-line now, people that can help. But, even greater than that, there's God, and He will provide you comfort and direction to find your way – the key is don't panic, but pray for guidance, seek help, make a plan- and know that you can and will get out of it."

"When I finally left my marriage, he told me that the world had moved on without me; that I didn't know the latest technology; that I would never own my own home, own a car, I would be nothing without him and when I decided to come to my senses, he would forgive me and take me back. Ha! We know how that turned out!"

"You did great Em, I know it was a struggle to say the

least. It took me a long time to realize that Joe didn't love himself. He had always been a loner; an abusive complainer with a negative attitude; a miserable person, and gambler that lost so much of our – my - hard earned money. His jealousy controlled me and alienated everyone around us, except his family. He was an amazing cook and caterer, I'll give him that, but he couldn't manage a business."

He would bring his taxes to an accountant who was willing to manipulate things and he received great big tax returns, but eventually things caught up with him and he was audited. Then he asked me to write a letter; straighten things out with taxes. I finally just said no; because if he had a decision to make between right and wrong, he always seemed to make the wrong one. I've always been responsible and have kept my credit in good standing.

We were in a new apartment, we both had car payments, insurance, bills, and all the other expenses that come with life. I began using the powerful word "No!" and put my foot down. I would pay the rent; that way I made sure that we had a roof over our heads, and I stopped handing my paychecks over to him. He could pay for all the other things like cable to watch sports and the phone bill to place bets. Gaining some sort of control over my finances, I was able to put money into my 401K and employee stock plan. It enabled me to do a little more of the things I wanted to do for myself, like buy clothes for work, or get out of the house on Sunday when football was on.

How did this bright, sunshine of a child get to this gray, sad place in life? Who was I becoming? Do I stay, or do I go? Do I divorce him or continue living this way? Will God be mad at me again? While questions choked my mind, Joe didn't let up. Still, I endured and kept working on my marriage.

Eight years into it, my son Beau arrived. I still cling to that moment when I took the pregnancy test, and as the positive plus sign appeared, there was no doubt or hesitation; I was going through with having my baby. In that instant I already loved this child. I told no one and went to the doctor to confirm it. Afterwards, I went to Hallmark, bought a Precious Moments figurine of an Angel holding a book in its arms that said, "Names for Babies." I got home to find Joe on the couch and "Free Falling" by Tom Petty on MTV. Holding my breath, I handed him the box and watched him as he unwrapped it; waiting for his reaction. It took a minute before it clicked but when it did, he was so happy! We felt like we were "Free Falling," and so excited to be having a child!

"Em, I had always wanted to be a stay at home mother if I could, so I cashed in what I had saved in stocks and gave it to Joe to open a business. He took on a young partner and had a large, beautiful, gourmet deli built while I was pregnant. With the security of the business, I thought I could stay home when the baby was born."

"Hmmm...that's interesting. I quit my job in the city before Bill and I got married. He took over a deli that he had financed and built, Food Festival, and I started managing it. It was called something else, but he renamed it. It had a huge pre-made dinner section, cheeses, fresh produce, pasta and meats. I used to drive to Yonkers to a little hole in the wall, family owned place L&J or L&B – can't remember, but they made the pasta fresh and I'd lug it back in a cooler. I knew nothing about run-

-ning a deli, much less gourmet premade foods!"

"J.B.? That's who we used! Where was your deli?"

"It's not there anymore. It was in Mt. Kisco I think there's a Staples or a CVS there now."

"Wait – that's where Joe's deli was. But it was called LaCarne Villa.

"That was the name! There was a jewelry store on the corner."

"Run by a real slime ball?"

"Yes! He kept trying to give me cheap jewelry to win me over."

"Tony? Arrogant Italian guy?"

"Yeah!"

"No way! He did the same with me! Just thought women could be bought; it worked for his wife! Oh my gosh Em! Your ex-husband built us the deli? I can't believe our paths didn't cross then! I was up and down the ladder stocking shelves; in the back, rolling meatballs and figuring out how to organize everything!"

"That's crazy! You were pregnant and built it, and a year later, I was pregnant and had to close it down. No wonder we always thought our kids were like brother and sister! By the way, the organization of everything, right down to the take-out containers, were perfect – should have realized it wasn't Joe or Bill's doing!"

"Em, when Beau was born, I was elated, but I found myself back at work. Joe had no discipline with money; the concept was over his head. His philosophy was, that if your food was good, the money would come – but so did the bills. He didn't mean to cause the demise of the deli, it was just too big of a place and the expenses were too high to cover."

"Bill didn't have any discipline either. He was, still is, a very talented designer and builder; that place was beautiful, but a lot happened that year. Two of his friends very unexpectedly passed away that year; the business declined, and he lost sight of things; of the people still in his life. Though I had never catered before, I learned pretty quickly. I enjoyed making beautiful, colorful platters of fruits and vegetables, but on my first delivery I dropped a huge tray of eggplant rollatini on the immaculate sidewalk of a home. Little old ladies going in for a Christening were pretty annoyed!

"Rollatini! Yikes couldn't have been something easier like the fruit platter!"

"Nope! I obviously like to complicate things! Despite the long hours and my efforts, Bill pretty much checked out, and running the business alone began to take its toll on me. We finally made the decision to close."

Beau wasn't an easy baby; didn't sleep through the night, needed to be held all the time, and didn't like much of anything other than a bottle for a very long time, but none of that mattered to me. When he was little, I would ask him "Beau, do you want me to carry you?" He'd lift his little arms for me to pick him up. When he started talking he'd say, "carry you" and put his hands up in the air, wanting me to carry him. I would carry him for as long as my arms could hold out. I'd sing songs and purposely mix up the words, like, "Hey diddle diddle, the cat and the fiddle, the dog jumped over the moon." Oh, silly me and we'd laugh and start over. I treasured every first time; the first time he ate baby food, or sat up on his own, took his first steps. I'd hold him as often as he as he wanted and talked to him all the time.

Working all day and up with the baby all night was very stressful. The walls to our one-bedroom apartment started closing in. Joe's jealous accusations hadn't subsided; they increased with his growing insecurities. While playing with our son, he created scenarios with Sesame Street characters. "Did Oscar the Grouch come play with Miss Piggy today?"

A healthy person allows and compensates for an unhealthy person. A healthy person takes responsibility for a child, for a home; but, eventually pays the consequences; both emotionally and physically. It takes its toll. Naturally having a child, I wanted to make my home and family a happy and healthy one. Joe eventually found another job and my mother cared for Beau while we worked. A little bit of hope shined through once again.

"Em, I wanted to make the marriage work. I worked around the clock to make ends meet, but what I received in return was "How long is it going to take you to get home? Where are you? Who were you with?"

My heart would race, and the blood would pound in my ears, as I drove like a crazy person trying to get through rush hour traffic to get home to avoid confrontation. I finally convinced him to go to marriage counseling. We each saw separate therapists, then met as a group. While I did the exercises given to us, he refused...all things were my fault in his eyes, therefore, he had nothing to fix...but me.

The unwarranted accusations and emotionally abusive words continued to attack me every day. I cried so often because my relationship with Joe was hurtful and exhausting. When would he ever see the truth? Or by my example see that I was a good mother to our son, a good wife to him? After more than a year of sessions, the therapists advised us that it just wasn't working. In their words, they "couldn't keep the pots from boiling over." Joe's stance was "See, I told you - it's you." There was no way to get through to him; I tried everything.

CHAPTER 11

WORDS ONCE SPOKEN

*"The tongue can bring death or life; those who love to
talk will reap the consequences." Proverb 18:21
"Above all else, guard your heart, for everything you
do flows from it." Proverb 4:23, NLT*

One of my favorite books in the Bible is the book of
Proverbs. There are 31 Proverbs and I highly recommend reading one a day, like a vitamin, and applying it to your life. What
you say over your life or someone else's life will have a positive
or negative effect, possibly even damaging consequences. Once
words are spoken they can't be taken back.

"Em, Joe's lies and torment held me down for a
long time and hurt me tremendously, but they could never
fully take root. My parent's love had already established a
strong foun-dation in my life, their words were engrained in
my heart and mind. Their love combined with my faith and
God's love for me, kept me from ever believing Joe's words.
They just weren't true, and I never accepted them. You are
responsible to guard your heart."

In *Proverbs 4:23, NLT God commands you to "...
above all else, guard your heart, for everything flows
out of it."* It could be the darkest day and you could be
going through a very difficult time or working on a boring
task, but if there's love in your heart, you'll be happy no
matter what the circumstance. The joy will spread into all
things. The opposite is true as well.

It could be a sunny beautiful day, but if your heart is in pain and emotions are damaged, you won't be happy no matter what the day brings. You'll feel lonely in a crowd. That's why God wants us to protect our hearts and make sure people are safe before we let them in.

Jesus says that it's impossible for someone to go through life without being offended; the greater the relationship, the harder the fall. A lot of people have been betrayed in relationships; thinking this is their life partner; best friend; or even in a parent and child relationship; a trusted teacher; a church member or in a job. That's also why most separations or divorces are the hardest; the hurt is incredibly strong after giving so much of your life to someone. That hurt can build walls of resentment, making it hard to trust again, to get past the anger and pain. That's why we need to take all the time we need to know that a person's words and actions line up. If they don't then they aren't safe for you. Guard your heart!

You can walk through life bitter and angry waiting for an apology or reconciliation that may never come. It's part of the trap – Satan will be right there trying to keep you from enjoying or living your life. Our minds can spin for years over how things happened. The good news is that we can be free of it all; we can be free of any type of bondage experienced in life. Whether we're the one hurt or the one who initiated the pain on another. Maybe you were the innocent one, a rape victim, molested, shamed, guilt ridden, ostracized, condemned – telling yourself you're not worth it anymore. Maybe you've fallen into depression or become a victim of oppression, anything that's been heavy or keeping you down, separated from the people you love.

84

It can cause you to become a workaholic, resentful, isolated; bring you down to bitter loneliness. Maybe you've worn out everyone around you by constantly reliving the pain or discussing it and you don't feel like you can attach to people. God does not want us to live this way. He wants to help us get past every single layer – every single one – so that there's nothing that the enemy can latch on to anymore. Be free of all our wounds – addictions, anxiety – all things that are not of God.

Since we were kids, we've said that 'sticks and stones can break our bones – but words can never hurt us,' but the truth of the matter is that words can cut deeper than a machete and leave a psyche severely damaged. The words we speak over another person's life are like seeds, and if seeds get rooted deep into the soul, watered and continually spoken over a person's life – they can become a product of those words. Like a garden, the weeds can take over and suffocate what was really meant to be. If a parent constantly puts a child down; or someone talks down to another; telling them that they're no good or will never mount to anything; or that they should be like someone else; amplifying what they see as a fault, they plant the seeds of discontent and failure. Even in a work environment; speaking to someone in a condescending tone can really do damage.

A woman that I worked with, was born to young parents that weren't married. Her father used to berate her with words "Can't you go somewhere else? Just get out of here?" Throughout her life, she remembered that, and she never felt like she was deserving of any real love from a man. From that young age, she carried her father's words in her heart.

∞

James 3:3-6, NLT

"3 When we put bits into the mouths of horses to make them obey us, we can turn the whole animal. 4 Or take ships as an example. Although they are so large and are driven by strong winds, they are steered by a very small rudder wherever the pilot wants to go. 5 Likewise, the tongue is a small part of the body, but it makes great boasts. Consider what a great forest is set on fire by a small spark. 6 The tongue also is a fire, a world of evil among the parts of the body. It corrupts the whole body, sets the whole course of one's life on fire, and is itself set on fire by hell."

∞

"Em, the words we speak determine the course of our lives and can affect the lives of others. They take root in our hearts, and like a bit in a horse's mouth, can pull us in different directions, determine the course of our lives, even change our true path. Words once spoken can't be taken back – they're already out. Like toothpaste out of a tube – you can't squeeze it back in."

"I love your analogies, but you're right; it's incredibly important to be careful of words before we speak them, especially to the ones we love; words can cut so deep whether we intend for them to or not."

"This doesn't mean that sometimes people don't need correction, you can say things in a loving way. But to continually put someone down or believe those words that someone may have used to put you down, is damaging. However, what God says about us is true, He will never lie to us."

We are His children; He knew us before we were ever created. He doesn't want us to live a life that is decaying by the negativity from someone's spoken words. It's so important to know His words. We can pray for the abuser, but, we should not be captive to them. Things will not change without the right motivation from all sides. To sincerely want to fix a situation, we have to get to the root of the problem and cut it out, otherwise, it will only fester and rise back to the surface. Any time that motivation isn't pure, isn't right and is just for the self, it won't work. If someone is doing something just to get what they want, or for the wrong reasons, and they're not willing to do it the right way, it will only repeat itself. It's hard! It takes practice to learn to change behavior and if it isn't with genuine willingness and self-discipline or self-control, it will resurface and continue in the painful circle that it revolves and lives in. God never wants His children to be abused.

CHAPTER 12
THE HOLY SPIRIT

"The helper (comforter, advocate, intercessor, counselor, strengthener, stand by), the Holy Spirit, whom the Father will send in my name (in my place, to represent me and act on my behalf), He will teach you all things. And He will help you remember everything that I have told you."
John 14:26, NASB

As I fell deeper into Joe's oppression, my mother finally came out of her depression. She started attending a charismatic church in Mt. Vernon and not only came so far out of her depression but was back stronger than ever. She started running a suicide hotline to help people at their lowest point. She got further involved with women's shelters and fundraisers. The transformation in her was so noticeably different, that when she asked us to join her at the Bible studies, we did. We were incredibly curious to see what changed her!

My father started attending Wednesday night Bible studies, and I eventually joined them. He gave me a book about the Holy Spirit and I started reading it, really wanting to understand who or what the Holy Spirit really was.

The scriptures are clear that the Father, Son, and the Spirit are equally eternal; one did not exist before the other, therefore, they always existed. In Genesis 1:26 God creates mankind in his own image. Although the Holy Spirit is a spirit without a human form, the traits or thoughts, are of both male and female. The Holy Spirit is gender neutral, but in most cases we refer to it as "He" or "It."

"Em, every time I went into St. Mary's, the tears would just flow. To this day, any church I go into, I cry."

"That's one reason I avoid church Jackie; I'm a mess. The tears just choke my throat and soak my face. If I go, I sit in the back where no one knows me, and I can slip out if it becomes too overwhelming."

"Em, you're not alone, just look around next time, others are in tears as well. While some cry, others feel such joy; all hopefully feel a sense of peace and healing. No, we don't have to go to a building to feel His presence, but we need the fellowship and the conversation with others to learn more about God. We have to open up our hearts and allow the Holy Spirit to come into our being – that's what makes us truly alive! Our soul has to agree to let Him in and 'clean house' – get rid of the clutter - everything that's built-up over time; everything and anything that's keeping us from being alive. We need each other; we need the Holy Spirit; we can't do it alone."

I realized that although I am always in the presence of the Holy Spirit, when I enter the church His presence and the sense of love for Him and His love for me is the strongest. Being in a church of worship, welcoming the Holy Spirit, and really feeling the presence of God is so powerful; I can't control the tears either and feel tremendously humbled.

People hold on to pride, self-righteousness, idolatries, and pay too much attention to the material things; other things are more important. He wants to clean up all those places in you that are hurting and holding you back. After you've accepted Jesus, the Holy Spirit lives inside you and is with you forever.

Your spirit quickens, and you know what it's like to be truly alive. Your physical body is a temple that holds both your soul and the Holy Spirit. In *John 14:26*, God shows us that *"The Comforter (Counselor, Helper, Intercessor, Advocate, Strengthener, Standby), the Holy Spirit, whom the Father will send in His name will teach us all things. And He will cause us to recall everything I have told you."* His love for you is as far as the East is to the West, and I don't mean the town that you're living in, I mean the ends of the universe. He is not a small God, He is the Holy Spirit – your counselor. He is wisdom that leads you to a better path– the advocate that will settle every case for you. He is the ultimate healer – there is no greater doctor that can heal your hurt and pain. It doesn't matter where you are or what you've done or not done. He just wants to love you and for you to know that you are loved in return. If you would just accept Him and let Him come in, it will change your life in ways you've never known or could imagine. You will see life through His eyes.

I'm certainly not perfect, but I have experienced His presence, His love and have let Him in. I have experienced so much and have gotten through it with Him and only with Him and now I see things the way He does. I feel such joy to see people loving one another, but my heart breaks when I see His people stuck in their bondage, broken and damaged. I'm compelled to help them find freedom and deliverance. I feel His presence and long to stay in it. That's why I cry. I feel the fullness of His love.

For ten years I endured a marriage full of ridicule, insults, suspicion, and verbal abuse. I continued attending the

Wednesday night Bible study classes with my parents. At the end of the class, the church offered a private prayer team that you could go to if you had a special request. I went to them and told them my situation with Joe, I had questions. "Would God be mad at me if I divorced him?" "Do I stay and put more into it?" I was questioning everything. They didn't give me the answers, but rather prayed with me for God to provide me with the answers.

Somehow, I convinced Joe to come to church with me one Sunday. As we walked up the stairs to the church, a gentleman said, "Hello Sister." That was it! Joe paid no attention to the message being taught that day and at the end of the service he accused me of being with that man and every other man who said hello to me on the way out. He still didn't get it!

CHAPTER 13
FEAR OF FLIGHT & THE STRENGTH TO MOVE ON

"But now you must also rid yourselves of all such things as these: anger, rage, malice, slander, and filthy language from your lips." Colossians 3:8, NIV

Ten years into our marriage, Duke died of a heart attack and Joe's mother decided she wanted to move in with us. Joe tried to justify it by saying that the extra money his mother would pay would help us financially. Unfortunately, Duke left nothing behind but gambling debts.

One morning, making meatballs and gravy for Sunday dinner, Joe came home from Atlantic City having lost our hard-earned money once again, and said that his mother had decided not to move in after all, and that it was my fault. The arguing got louder and angrier.

Marriage is not supposed to be a battlefield. There's a book in the Bible, Song of Songs that describes marriage as two armies marching together, helping each other and defending one another. Not fighting each other, but rather side by side to guard and protect their relationship from those that can destroy it. There must be mutual respect to not allow anyone or anything to alter the relationship. Marriage is a garden that should be carefully cultivated and thoroughly enjoyed the way God intended. My marriage was so far from that and I knew that I could no longer fix it.

"Em, Beau was only 2-years old and as sweet as he could be. When he cried out "Stop!" I knew at that moment, that if I stayed, he would grow up with the same damaging effects that his father had grown up with seeing his parents fight."

"Abuse of any kind can grip deeper than we realize; we can carry it with us unknowingly, or unwillingly to acknowledge it and stop it. Sometimes, someone has to break the chains of past generations Jackie."

"Duke never asked for help or wanted to change his life, or free himself from his addictions. Joe's mother wouldn't change and stayed in that marriage despite the abuse. Joe would never truly love himself or change his addictions and insecurities. BUT! Beau and I had a future and a purpose. I finally realized that I couldn't fix them, no matter how hard I tried — but I could change the future for my son and for me."

It had taken ten years for me to finally shout out that I'd had enough of the accusations and hated how I had been treated for so many years. I refused to be treated like that any longer and wasn't going to allow my sweet, innocent little child to endure that kind of life.

Joe left furious, slamming the door behind him. My heart pounded as I tossed a few things into bags and took only what was necessary; Beau's birth certificate, important documents, things that would be hard to replace. I threw dresser drawers into the car and grabbed my son with the clothes on our backs and drove, shaking, to my parent's house. Material things could be replaced but our mental well-being couldn't.

I had left Joe twice before and went back, believing that he was sorry, and we would try again to make it work this time; it was okay to go back and try again. We should try and should want to work things out, especially a marriage, it's a divine union. But at some point, you need to make the But at some point, you need to make the decision; be honest with yourself and find the strength to move on. For me, nothing changed then, and it wasn't going to change now. I could no longer allow the problems of the last ten years to fall on my son. It was enough that I endured it, but he didn't have to. It was heartbreaking, but I knew that if I had waited and stayed together for the sake of our child, it would only prolong the pain and strengthen the damage that was already occurring.

My son loved his father, and though it was very hard on him, I knew the damage would only be greater if we stayed. Through his tears and crying for his father, and wanting to go home, my heart was breaking for my little Beau, but I drove on.

CHAPTER 14
LIFE BY SPREADSHEET

"For which of you desiring to build a tower does not first sit down and count the cost whether he has enough to complete it? Otherwise, when he has laid a foundation, he is not able to finish, all those who see it begin to mock him saying, "This man began to build and was not able to finish." Luke 14: 28-30, ESV

Our first Thanksgiving without him was strange, but good; I had a supportive family and great friends to turn to. But, it was still an incredibly frightening time in my life. Joe and I didn't have a legal separation agreement, so there were many unsettling and fearful visitations. When Christmas came, I was terrified that he would try to take Beau and not bring him back. He told me that if I came back, he would give me back my possessions. He promised the perfect fairy tale life and all that I had hoped for; "Please come back, I want to work this out with you. I'll give you everything you ever wanted." I didn't cave so he reverted to "I'm going to take him away from you; you're no good; your family's no good; where you're living is no good..."

That same abusive behavior began to show itself again, but, it only made me stronger and reinforced my decision and actions. At that point, I knew that I had to set a budget, find a way, and save up for the day that my son and I could be on our own. Joe was still in denial and thought that I would come running back to him when I had enough. But my journey had already started, disciplined, budgeted, and focused.

With nothing other than our clothes, I left Joe; I was willing to work hard to create a new life for my son and me. Though Beau was only two, I knew I had to think long-term and focus on what I wanted for us. I wasn't crazy about the school system in my parent's area, so settling there wasn't going to be an option. Working for one of the largest telecommunication companies in the U.S., I asked my boss for overtime helping another department. While Beau slept, I took on a part-time job working nights and every other weekend at a catering hall. Mom watched him, which was a tremendous help; but, I never took advantage of that. As soon as he turned three, I paid for nursery school a few days a week.

Dad and I used to sit downstairs in my grandmother's apartment with her and talk about stocks and investments. He always wanted me to be successful and always had a unique way of explaining meaningful wisdom, with stories and analogies. Still a chain smoker at this point in his life, he would hold up a pack of Pall Mall cigarettes in his right hand and say "Jacquelyn, this is your goal. If you want to move Beau into a comfortable, secure environment, don't kid yourself that money isn't important – there's security in money and having a good quality of life. In his left hand, he would hold up his cigarette lighter and say "On the other hand, you may feel like buying more clothes, shoes, or other things that you don't necessarily need, you will be detoured from your goal. No Detours!"

His message was simply that when you have something you want to accomplish, it takes a lot of effort to plan and prepare. His favorite example was of two old ladies who lived in the east. They dreamed of retiring on the beautiful island of Haw-

-aii. When they finally retired, they packed up and headed west to fulfill their lifelong dream. They planned and prepared but settled somewhere in California; they never made it to the beautiful beaches and lush tropics of Hawaii. They never got to really enjoy the fullness of their destination and dreams. Get the fullness of where God wants you to be, where you want to be, don't settle. He kept emphasizing "No detours! No detours!"

While his anecdotes were entertaining, they came from a place of knowing. I witnessed him go from hallucinations when he struggled with alcoholism, through detox, losing his job, losing everything; to being delivered from alcoholism and finding his way to once again being gainfully employed. He started providing for his family again, and not only saving money, but making wise investments that secured his future and that of his children's.

I didn't want to live where they did and wanted a different life for my son. That was my driving force. I also knew that I didn't want to rely on others and that I needed a disciplined plan of action.

Satan puts so many obstacles in our lives, but God's grace aligns good people in our lives to counter act that. Throughout my life, I made great friends and held on to them; some from St. Anthony's, others from work, some by paths simply crossing. They were God's gift to me. They helped me to keep moving forward and gave me the added strength I needed through the hardest times. Rosa worked with me at one of the world's most prominent beverage companies; a strong personality that was there for me when Beau was born, and when I bought my first home. Anna from high school sat and did crafts and couponing with me; her son Christopher is my Godson; he and Beau are like cousins.

Barbara, Diana and I worked together and developed not only our friendship, but a strong support system that helped me get through the divorce. Both single parents, they were like big sisters and they made the time to listen to me. Diana lived in Dobbs Ferry, a wonderful little town with a great school system. Her apartment complex had fireplaces, a pool and had a great neighborhood feel to it. Barbara and her son moved into the complex as well.

My heart was set that my son would grow up in a small, safe, clean town along the Hudson River, with an excellent school system and receive a good education. I wanted him to make friends that he could keep and grow up with, and not have to be uprooted again; or have obstructions in his life. I loved my neighborhood growing up and wanted him to have the kind of childhood that I started out with. This complex was where we needed to be, and I prayed that God would make it happen. I also knew that I needed to have a plan to get there so I created a savings system and lived my life by spreadsheet.

"Life by spreadsheet? No way Jackie! That's exactly what I did."

"Em, it works - I still live by it."

"I do too!"

"It's important to set a plan for your finances. You can't keep track of it in your head; you have to write it down and make it visible, otherwise you end up living paycheck to paycheck without a chance to build and save."

No detours! I needed a system, so I could budget and

save. Just thinking about the bills, the rent, the debt from my divorce, wasn't going to get anything paid, it would only cause more stress. I had dreams that I wanted to achieve. Seeing it in black and white, in front of me, kept me focused and made it possible to get through it.

Mental and financial stress are heavy burdens. Life by spreadsheet was the only way I could keep focused on my goals and see it taking shape. It really wasn't hard to create, and at the end of the day, it gave me peace of mind. I could see what I had, what I needed, and how to get there.

You don't have to be an Excel wiz; you don't even have to have a computer! Get a journal. Across the top I had the months of the year; under each month, a starting checking account balance; the line below that for other income from paychecks and then I totaled it out to give me the net income for the month. To the left were all expenses broken down in two sections. One for expenses directly paid from the checking account and the other for expenses paid directly from my credit card.

The credit card earned points or rewards, but the limit was paid off at the end of the month. That built good credit and gave me some perks. The balance that I strived for and achieved, was that my combined expenses never exceeded my total income.

I was able to budget a little each month for vacations, factoring in points and reward savings from the credit card. I remembered to pay myself by wire into a separate money market savings account and began to contribute to my 401K plan which was pre-tax from my salary. Honestly, you don't miss the money that comes out. I contributed to the employee stock purchasing program at 15% below market price but cashed in at market price at the end of each month. That was a forced gain. My mind was fully disciplined with no detouring. I became creative with 0% credit card transfers knocking off debt and utilizing revolving credit accounts. Short term CD's were popular, so I made minimum payments of $25 a month and at the end of the CD, with the term interest of 5-7% and no risk, I'd immediately return the banks money and refinance the debt. Most people wouldn't do this – but I did. Some of these methods may not apply today, but there are other creative ways to make your money work for you and grow. When you ask God to be your partner, and respect your money, He'll put ideas in your mind and keep you focused. Watch your money! Be a good steward of it. You know what you need; figure out what's in front of you that could help you.

With overtime and a second job, it took two years to move out of my parent's home. It's amazing the drive that you get when you become a lioness for your child and your life. One summer, I got a vending license and sold glow lights at the 4th of July firework event. "Glow lights – get your glow lights here!" My sister and I took Beau with us to fields where families set up their picnics with chairs and blankets, and the kids would come running over with their parents to buy them. That money paid for Beau's summer camp year after year, and Beau had a great time playing and seeing all the kids.

On weekends, I would review the children's section of the newspaper to see what was going on and planned fun things for us to do. Sometimes it was as simple as going to

McDonalds to jump in the ball pit or meet up with friends and go to the park, but we always did something. The Bronx Zoo was his favorite.

"You sound like your Mom."

"Thanks, Em. I learned from the best! And from my dad too; his eccentricity rubbed off on me. Beau and I had a lot of adventures."

I envisioned how I wanted our new apartment to look and forecasted for every piece of new furniture, carpeting, tile, window treatments, appliances; every new dish, glass, towel, pots and pans. Within the first year of living by spreadsheet, I was able to start buying items I wanted on my list, usually on sale at a really good price and with a coupon! I would then take them off the forecasted list, adjust for what I spent, which reduced my savings – but I had allowed and saved for that spend. I kept the items in my parent's attic; it was my way of knowing I was really doing this!

Beau's personality was developing; he was brilliant, adorable, very sensitive and caring, yet somewhat shy; but talkative if he knew you. When I introduced him to someone he'd say, "I am Beau, B-E-A-U" and he'd spell it out. Then, anticipating the next question of "How old are you?" he would say, "and I am four." If he got to the third sentence, he'd tell them that he liked animals. He really loved every single animal. We always had lots of imaginary ones with us: Stripes the Tiger and Motor the Lion pulled our car on the highway like a chariot. There were lots of cool dogs that ran along the side as we drove; Jeremy was the father of the dogs. We studied and read wild life encyclopedia, zoo magazines and he learned the different species, bone structures, muscle and respiratory systems. Very smart, if I do say so myself!

Just two months before his 4th birthday, with diligent effort and a lot of prayer, God's grace opened the door to the apartment I had prayed for. It was in a small, safe and clean, river town along the Hudson, with an excellent school system. Just what I had asked Him for. It was a great little one-bedroom apartment with a fireplace, a swimming pool and everything that I had envisioned, and debt free. With all the stuff I had stored in the attic loaded into the truck, and the last details like carpet installation and our new furniture delivery complete, Beau and I drove off with our chariot of imaginary animals, as my parents and sister saluted me good-bye.

God gives us or shows us a way out. He puts people in our lives that can help. It's up to us to reach out and take their hand. It took me time to do what I needed to, so I moved in with my parents; made a budget and stuck to it! Make a commitment to yourself, stay strong and focused – but you need a plan – No Detours!

After a lot of hard work and gaining knowledge of the Settlement department, I noticed quite a few discrepancies in the international voice traffic division. Country vs. country we had been losing money. I investigated, and later created a process and system for recouping anywhere from $20 to $48 million dollars a year. Hard work and dedication paid off and I transitioned into a completely new role and no longer needed to keep the second job. Beau and I were off to a great start. The sense of being on our own with no more negative energy was liberating. My son was everything to me and I had created a new home for us.

Time eventually proved that in situations like this, there are often two types of parents – healthy and unhealthy. The unhealthy parent tends to manipulate the young mind, which can still cause damage. "Mommy was the one who took you away. It's her fault that the family isn't together."

Beau was with me twelve straight days; his father's visitation was every other weekend. My entire life, I had never been alone. I had either lived with my parents, was in a relationship, or was married. This was the first time I had every other weekend to myself. It was nice! It was healthy for me to finally have my own time to enjoy. God continued to bless me with great friends who loved me and supported me through the difficult times of my marriage and divorce and I greatly appreciated them. I was able to go out, not worry about what I wore, who I talked to, and was able to do anything I wanted to do, with the people I cared about. Finance and investments intrigued me, and I started taking college courses through an accelerated program for accounting and taxation.

Joe took Beau on nice vacations, bought him toys, but he never paid child support or a penny to help; yet he was able to take him to Disney. Our son needed clothes, food, shelter, child care – not Mickey Mouse and gifts. I still had the responsibility of paying for everything.

Through it all, I never spoke negatively to my son about his father and supported their relationship – with caution. Beau had and continues to have a relationship with both of us. He's just as close with his dad today as he is with me. That's not to say that the relationships are perfect, I am very mindful of the pitfalls. As he started getting older, I thought it best to let him figure things out on his own.

Joe called one weekend when Beau was with him and wanted to know if I was down and out and asked if I was feeling lonely. My answer – "Nope! I'm great! Have a nice day!" For the first time in my life I truly had freedom. It was a time of celebration – a victory. The next few years of my journey continued to be lessons learned, and I discovered a lot more about the world, especially the spiritual world.

Life was good, but I was losing my way

CHAPTER 15
NOT ALL RELATIONSHIPS ARE OF GOD

"For we wrestle not against flesh, but against principalities, against powers, against the rulers of darkness of this world, against spiritual wickedness in high places." Ephesians 6:12, NIV

With my new-found freedom, I was thankful to be free and alive; to be successful and financially stable. Life started going great and my goals were being achieved. I was promoted at work and doing very well; making money, buying clothes, taking vacations, and enjoying time with my friends. I was having fun and living the good life.

When Beau was with his father, and only when he was away, I started partying at the beach, smoking a little pot here and there. I was still a responsible parent and my son remained the most important person in my life, but Jesus had started fading into the background. I still had the connection to Him but was getting further and further away from Him. I was testing out things that I hadn't tried before; dating several guys at the same time; becoming a player, becoming "worldly." I was healthy, tan, in great shape and turned plenty of heads in a bikini as I broke free from the chains that had bound me for so long. I gave into it all and lived it for many years, until I really started seeing the dark side of life and people. God had faded into the distance; life was good, but I was losing my way. Dating was something I wanted to happen again in my life. I was a loving person with the hope that there was someone out there for me.

Like so many others, I hoped to find my soul-mate; the one that was my partner for the rest of my life; we would be attracted to one another, in love and best friends; we could work through anything together and be there for each other no matter what. No abuse, no fighting, no betrayals.

At twenty-nine, I left Joe and started enjoying being myself. As my circle of friends grew, the real beauty was that those great friendships became family.

Relationships can be wonderful and full of light, like the ones I have with my close friends. But, not all relationships are of God. It wasn't until I became a minister and started teaching the Deliverance series that I truly understood or realized that there are fragmented spirits all around us. Spirits that can attach to us in ways without us even realizing it, or until we're too deep into a relationship. There are unholy hosts and the enemy has many different levels of demons and principalities that he uses against us.

Over the last few years I've learned a lot about these evil spirits: the Spirits of Jezebel, Absalom, Ahab and Reprobate to name a few. All are very real. But, because we haven't been told about their existence, we aren't able to identify the traits in those that cross our path or enter or lives. We may recognize the evil or damage that they cause, but until we can put a name to a problem – or an evil spirit - we write it off as a character flaw or a one-off situation.

Psychiatrists classify, analyze and diagnose personality types or disorders; like a person with empathy, or apathy; or with passive-aggressive or passive-passive tendencies. There are good people that have emotional issues that can be treated and live a good life. But, there is darker psychological biblical classification for demonic forces like the narcissist, the socio-path, or the psychopath. For these forces, the Bible says that there is no hope of recovery.

If we can begin to identify these characteristics and understand that they are part of a larger conspiracy, then we can begin to heal and move away from them and the damage they cause.

A few years ago, I met Ron in the fashion industry. He fell for Jennifer, a wealthy woman, and started a relationship. They had a lot in common; both enjoyed being well dressed, creative, smart, and attractive and lived together for a while, eventually getting married. Together they opened a business and took on a CPA, Brian as a partner. Jennifer invested most of the money to start the business, but allowed Ron to be the buyer, seller and basically the wheeler and dealer.

Over time, their partner who managed the accounts, discovered that Ron had been stealing from the business. When he questioned him, the answer was always a story that never added up, nor did the numbers. Brian had also invested in their joint venture and needed to protect his interests. He had no choice but to take it to the Supreme Court.

Ron retained a high-powered attorney to fight the charges and lied through his teeth. He racked up eighty-thousand dollars in legal fees and over two-hundred in back taxes and penalties, but Brian's numbers were proven and didn't lie. The judge ruled in Brian's favor. Ron had to pay back Brian, his lawyer, the I.R.S., and the New York State Tax Commission. His debt was well over a million dollars and the business was forced to shut down with a bad reputation.

Ron claimed bankruptcy, was no longer employable, and could not maintain the lifestyle he and Jennifer had become accustomed to. With the Spirit of Jezebel, Jennifer had all their marital properties illegally transferred into her maiden name but did not divorce him. They lived in a 50/50 no fault state; a divorce would require her to give 50% of her assets to him, and she was not about to give up any of her wealth.

Since she was able to provide for herself, she emotionally and financially checked out of the relationship. As corrupt as he was, his new means of living were the same as his old ways of living, just no longer in the store-front, but on the street. He continued to be a scammer. Jennifer didn't care how he obtained an income just as long as money was coming in and she could control it.

Why is this important today? The Bible tells us in *Matthew 12:43 that "...there are levels of wickedness in Satan's kingdom."* Jennifer was the principality of the demonic Spirit of Jezebel, while Ron was the principality of the demonic Spirit of Ahab.

Jezebels operate by playing games that are mentally damaging; tears down families, marriages, businesses, churches - all that is important. Don't kid yourself into thinking that all people are good. They aren't, and these spirits do exist. Without question, the Spirit of Jezebel is one of the most hated, nastiest, most cunning and seductive spirits in Satan's hierarchy.

The Spirit of Jezebel is never wrong or sorry and can be male or female. People with this spirit may say things like, "I'm sorry you feel like that," but they will not ever admit that they were the cause. They don't see it that way and it's near impossible for them to change. But, there are ways to recognize this spirit. Their control is a form of self-worship; they will not violate their pride to apologize and will take credit for everything except their wrong actions or behavior.

This spirit will use others to accomplish their agendas; let them do the dirty work then appear innocent as if they had nothing to do with the corruption, damage, or pain that was caused. They need to control information and be the first to know; dive deep into the thick of people's lives promising never to tell anyone your secret; spin webs of drama; play both sides of a story; withhold information. It gives them a sense of power, while they actively gossip your personal business.

In relationships, issues arise that matter to the heart and can be resolved. But, Jezebels are convincing liars and will control the conversation, twist the situation so much that you will never get to the root of a problem. They are charming enough to make you believe them and will look you in the eye while manipulating you. They will pressure you to do things, and over time will make you feel like you don't have the ability to make choices. They sow seeds of discord using half-truths to devalue others.

This spirit doesn't need you, but will hang out with you, lavish you with long flowery flattering complements; build up your self-esteem for as long as it takes to butter you up; until you cooperate enough to conform to their needs. They'll convince you to give them money, your contacts, take jobs from you. They are users, who will do anything to get what they want. You mean nothing to them at all; just a means to an end.

Ron embodied The Spirit of Ahab, a split man who appeared efficient, strong, and charismatic; even influential. He manipulated into a greater scheme of corruption and allowed a Jezebel spirit to hijack his authority for it to be achieved. When caught in a vice-grip of lies and deception, this spirit will repent, but only with mere words. There is no sincerity, there's no change of behavior. Pathetically, he will change the facts, set others up to take the blame and will never take responsibility for his actions.

Absalom is another spirit that can be identified in someone that appears rational yet has deep rooted irrational secrets that they act out. Excellent at camouflaging bitterness and hidden agendas for revenge, they rebel against authority; appear to be your friend; have an inflated justification or exaggerated sense of self and reinforce that their way is the right way. They don't act with a pure heart, are not loyal and they're not your friend.

They are masters of betrayal with the purpose of taking over and destroying others. If part of a family, they may be the sibling that will crush the others and take more. They become corrupt figures of authority who will battle you in law suits; ruin businesses and governments; corrupt sports teams; music bands and anything that requires a leader, coach, teacher, or department head.

These evil spirits boldly remove God from our lives as they work to destroy His kingdom.

The last one I want to share with you is probably the most damaging, the Spirit of Reprobate. These are sociopaths and psychopaths. There is no coming back to God, for they follow the father of lies. They have no feelings of sorrow or remorse. They are con-men and women who will twist your words, play mind games and cause chaos. They know how to bend the truth so that their lies are believable. It's a great strategy, the same one that Satan used in the Garden of Eden.

∞

Mark 3:28-29, NASB

"Truly I say to you, all sins shall be forgiven the sons of men, and whatever blasphemies they utter; but whoever blasphemes against the Holy Spirit never has forgiveness, but is guilty of an eternal sin..."

∞

There's no hope for one that possesses the Spirit of a Reprobate because they blasphemy against the Holy Spirit. While they do know that the Holy Trinity exists: The Father, The Son and The Holy Spirit, the reprobate denies and continuously resists the power of the Holy Spirit and chooses to follow Satan. God already knows that the heart of a reprobate is too hard and that they will never change, so he rejects them and gives them up to a reprobate mind; sealing their demise. If God said have nothing to do with them then who are we to try?

Romans 1:28-31, ESV

"...since they did not see fit to acknowledge God, God gave them up to a debased mind to do what ought not to be done. They were filled with all manner of unrighteousness, evil, covetousness, malice. They are full of envy, murder, strife, deceit, maliciousness. They are gossips, slanderers, haters of God, insolent, haughty, boastful, inventors of evil, disobedient to parents, foolish, faithless, heartless, ruthless."

I have endured the full range of how a sociopath operates; and the lies they create. If you encounter one, I would advise you to run as far as you can. Their biggest fear is that you will figure them out and they can't control you any longer or that you will expose them. They will want to destroy you like their father, the devil, as they devolve into being his children. But God provides His children with the armor to warfare against them. I learned that I had to put my armor on every day without fail.

Ephesians 6:10-18, NIV "Finally, be strong in the LORD and in his mighty power. Put on the full armor of God, so that you can take your stand against the devil's schemes. For our struggle is not against flesh and blood, but against the rulers, against the authorities, against the powers of this dark world and against the spiritual forces of evil in the heavenly realms. Therefore put on the full armor of God, so that when the day of evil comes, you may be able to stand your ground, and after you have done everything, to stand. Stand firm then, with the belt of truth buckled around your waist, with the breastplate of righteousness in place, and with your feet fitted with the readiness that comes from the gospel of peace. In addition to all this, take up the shield of faith, with which you can extinguish all the flaming arrows of the evil one. Take the helmet of salva-tion and the sword of the Spirit, which is the word of God."

Get into the habit of reading this scripture out loud so that you are protected and can fight against evil and those that come against you. It's important to wear your spiritual armor every day. My hope is that through what I am sharing with you, you will begin to really recognize these fragmented spirits of of Satan. We do not have to remain tied to one; we don't need to carry them with us throughout our lives; but we do need to recognize and accept that these entities exist and are of the enemy. Strengthen your relationship with God and learn to wear the armor that He's given you and you will break free from the ties that bind you. Don't dance with demons.

CHAPTER 16
SPIRITUAL WARFARE

"Be self-controlled and alert. Your enemy the devil prowls around like a roaring lion looking for someone to devour." 1 Peter 5:8, NIV

It's important to recognize that Satan exists and has the ability to roam the earth and recognize weakness to use against us as he steals our joy; our lives. He traps us by putting obstacles in our way and keeps us trapped through shame, guilt, condemnation, addiction, depression, fear and anxiety. His mission is to destroy and condemn us to an eternal hell. Death is not just life ended, never to wake up, it is a severe, never ending eternal torment for those that follow him. *"The thief comes only to steal and kill and destroy. I came that they may have life and have it abundantly" John 10:10.* However! It is even more important to recognize and accept that God exists and when Jesus died for us His blood redeemed us. Our sins died with Him on the cross and when we accept Him, His blood covers us with His righteousness. Satan hates that we receive righteousness through Jesus and therefore does everything he can to play on our weakness, but he cannot penetrate through the blood of Christ. When we accept Jesus, it's His blood that protects us and helps us to fight the battles that are brought before us. The Bible is clear, we live in a world with supernatural forces working against us, but we are also given the armor to stand against them; not on our own, but by drawing on the Word of God and relying on His power. *"Truly he is my rock and my salvation; he is my fortress, I will never be shaken" Psalm 62:2*. Hope and basic prayers are not sufficient to overcome the strongest attacks; we have to be strategic bibli-cally and spiritually as we warfare against any strongholds the enemy has on us or on someone we care about.

"Em, you remember Shane. He had that amazing restaurant that Miriam designed."

"The one that reminded us of Cheers – at first."

"Yeah...at first."

I have an amazing Christian friend, Miriam, who does interior design work for restaurants and clubs, and even homes for professional ball players and teams like the Yankees, Mets and Knicks. She often pulls me into her work to assist or for my opinion. I love helping her! She had been working on a new restaurant and bar on the Long Island Sound. She created such a great theme for a very cool BBQ place. After about nine months working with Shane, the owner, she started playing cupid and wanted us to meet.

The grand opening was around Christmas time and she was pushing me to go. I had heard so much about the restaurant, him, and all the work she had done, and I wanted to see it, so I went. She's amazing! It looked cozy and charming with wide, dark wood window panes, the snow freshly fallen along the ledge and corners. Reminiscent of a pirate ship, we walked up the ramp like entrance, through rustic pillars as if walking onto a boat. Inside, the lighting was warm and welcoming and had a family feel.

Shane was just as much fun as she had said he was. They showed me around, asking my advice, and I was happy to give it – sure, twist my arm.

Although I had a full-time job, I started dropping in every few days to help and hang out. After several weeks, I found myself there more often, and at the end of the night, he and I would stay up late and talk. I was having a good time and getting to know the regular customers and they were getting to know me. I was becoming part of his life, involved in the restaurant and coming up with ideas. It had a good feel to it and I was really falling for him.

He had a woman working there that he'd known for a long time, Janie. She treated me okay at first, but I could tell she wasn't very happy with me being around.

Over the holidays, Shane and I decided to deliver food to homeless shelters. He said that "It warms the heart." The late nights continued and eventually we started dating. Of course, my overly protective friends, including Emel, all came out to interrogate him, and he treated everyone really well. They unanimously fell in love with him and approved. Believe me – they came and checked him out - third degreed him while watching every move he made to ensure they didn't miss anything! He won them all over without even trying.

Miriam started designing two apartments above the restaurant; one for him, one for Janie. The views overlooking the Sound were gorgeous and he based the décor around my suggestions and choices. It made me feel special. Miriam shared with me that he said he loved me and that I was the one.

Janie didn't feel quite the same! To say that she didn't

like the fact that he was falling in love with me was an understatement! She had been his friend for over ten years; they had lived together and though she had no financial investment, he made her a partner in the new business. An illegal Irish immigrant, she got free room and board, and in exchange, she was supposed to manage the business. When, and if, it made a profit above his investment, she would get a portion. However, her real intention was to marry him; it was the only way for her to stay in the country. Willing to do anything to make that happen, she wasn't about to let me stand in the way.

My birthday is the day after St. Patrick's Day. I took a short trip to visit my friends Andrea and Phil in Ft. Lauderdale. Janie threw a St. Patrick's Day party at the restaurant and took full advantage of Shane by passing him shots and encouraging him to drink along with everyone else. The more she could keep him drinking, the better for her; but worse for the business, for him, for us. I was an absolute threat.

When I came back, he surprised me with a wonderfully romantic evening in the city and took me to Radio City to see Seal in concert. He asked if I wanted a drink, then got us both one. At that point, I had no idea that he had a drinking problem and had only been sober for a year and half his entire life; he had begun to spiral down and out of control.

It wasn't always easy for him to get out of the restaurant, but one night, he wanted to be alone with me and took me to a very fine, Italian restaurant. He really wanted to wine and dine me, impress me and make me feel special; he was becoming friends with the owners and they pulled out all the stops to provide a memorable evening.

During the dinner, his mother called from Florida; she was planning on coming to New York for the summer. He couldn't wait for us to meet and had been telling her about me since he met me. He passed the phone for me to say hello; we were both excited to be talking to each other. I was telling her that we were out for a special dinner and having a glass of wine.

Very sternly, she said "Jackie, he cannot have any wine! Listen to me. No alcohol can pass his lips. Do you understand what I mean? Don't let him know I'm telling you any of this honey." In the same breath, she warned me that Janie was an alcoholic too and that she didn't know if she could trust her. She was coming to New York to assess the situation.

About three months into our relationship, his stress level had escalated. As part owner of a popular restaurant in Manhattan, he traveled back and forth trying to balance everything. Since starting the new place, he was stretched thin financially and mentally, and his partners wanted him out; he felt hurt and rejected.

Easter was spent together, and I introduced him to my father. They hit it off, Dad really liked him. But later that spring, Shane started sounding like an Alzheimer's patient; twisted in thoughts. Living on top of his own bar, he had fallen off the wagon. I tried to talk sense into him and reached out to my dad for advice and asked questions. Does Shane realize that somethings wrong? Does he know what he's doing? My father would say "Yes, he knows what he's doing." My father was around 40 when he got sober, Shane was around 40 and I really believed that he could be successful and get sober like my dad had.

We prayed for him, and Dad would give me the no nonsense side of it. He would say "No B.S. – don't B.S. me or him, don't let him B.S. you – make the commitment and don't be afraid to call it what it is." Someone had to tell him that he was an alcoholic, he was losing his business and had to decide what he was going to do. Dad was adamant that we weren't helping him by pretending that everything was okay – we had to face the truth and we had to tell him the truth.

Shane's mother arrived, but rather than being forth-coming or forceful like she had been on the phone, she simply said that there was nothing to be ashamed of in going to AA, yet, she didn't push him. She arranged for Tom, his cousin to come and speak with him; she did what she knew. Tom had helped him get sober the first time, but it was by force, not choice. Still, I felt like help was on the way and that between the three of us, we hoped that we could get him to admit that he needed help. Dad stood his ground and reminded me that by not acknowledging that Shane was an alcoholic, was not help-ing him. We had to come straight out with it and call it what it was! My dad had turned his life around, why couldn't he do it too? He did it before; I thought he could love me enough to do it again. Stubborn, pride and arrogance; he claimed there was nothing wrong with him. *Proverb 16:18 says "pride precedes a disaster, and an arrogant attitude precedes a fall."*

Janie continued her antics. She would come over to watch TV; his excuse was that his TV was better than hers. She began leaving her underwear on his bed, the ex-cuse this time was that the washer and dryer were in his apartment, so their clothes got mixed up sometimes.

One morning, I found glue in my shampoo, another time she broke a glass in the shower, and when I mentioned it, he said a lightbulb had broken – but there was no light in the shower – and why would she even be in his shower? He had just built a nice apartment for her next door with a perfectly good bathroom. Her jealousy kept rearing its ugly head, but he continuously dismissed it.

I told him my concerns and that I didn't trust her or the situation, so he dropped her off to her sister's house, but of course she came right back. She would crawl into bed with him, supposedly after he had fallen asleep; two drunk people that claimed they weren't doing anything. He always had an excuse for her. There was always a reason why she wasn't going to leave, so I made the decision to leave instead.

I watched all the sharks take advantage of him. Yes, sharks surrounded his ship. His investment broker was shorting his positions and he was losing a lot of money very quickly. I built a compliance case to try and help him. Remember what I said about the trouble you can get into if you go that direction? You think you're so cool when you're drunk, and everyone loves you. That's what he thought. But his charm wasn't going to save him this time.

Though I was very shaken by his drinking and Janie's actions, I put a lot of time into talking with his family and watching over the situation. Miriam and I prayed a lot for him. Though she had never experienced alcoholism, she quickly became educated as she remained attached to the situation. There were times where she talked to him and he seemed normal, but he wasn't.

Friends and family tried talking to him and tried to take him away from the restaurant and away from Janie; but she held on tight as his drinking buddy. During one of their drun-

-ken nights at the bar, I heard that she said to him 'Well, I guess since everyone's gone, it's just you and me," then she asked him to marry her.

It finally dawned on him that I was right in what I was saying. He decided to get away to an island with someone he respected, with the intent to get sober. That was only half of his battle; she did everything under the sun to stand in his way. Miriam arrived to take him to the airport, but Janie stood in the way and insisted that she couldn't handle the restaurant alone and gave every reason why she was afraid – she hid the ticket and created numerous obstacles.

He did finally go on the trip, but sadly it didn't make any difference. When he returned, he spent a fortune on billboards and advertising; but Janie had run the business so far into the ground, that there was no coming back. The décor became over-whelming and tacky; things didn't match. Though the restaurant remained open, we watched the ship style restaurant that was once like Cheers – a welcoming, comfortable place where the dark wood and seating was cozy and warm - slowly turn to darkness and sink into an abyss of drunkenness.

Miriam and I started to warfare against his stronghold. Hearing her speak scripture started bringing it all back to me as we prayed for him. As hard as we tried, we helplessly watched him plummet into darkness - a beautiful person, but he couldn't resist the colorful bottles. Though I didn't have a drinking prob-lem, I couldn't be around it anymore. I hated what it had done to him – what he had allowed it to do to him. There was nothing more we could do; it devastated me, I finally had to walk away. "Em, at some point, I realized that I just wanted to fix him. Yes, I saw the flaws, the problems he faced, his addictions, but I really thought that I could help him."

"We can't fix people Jackie. They have to want to do it themselves. But more importantly, they need to recognize and accept their issues or weaknesses. A lot of people live in denial. I know you and Miriam tried hard; but until a person decides that they want to change, they won't – they can't."

I really fell for Shane and was traumatized by it all, it took me a very long time to get back into socializing and going out. I knew that I needed to get back to church, I was broken. Though I continued to pray for him and warfare against the stronghold that alcohol and Janie had on him, I finally recognized that I was still using all my energy on him. I had to turn it over and leave it fully in God's hands. My father turned himself around, so I think that's why I had such hope that he could as well. But that hope diminished and I turned inward, just wanting to be with God. It was my time to heal, both physically and emotionally.

One afternoon, walking through a gift shop, I purchased a healing CD and started listening to it at night. It spoke about the promises of God and what they meant.

For five long years I had endured back pain. After two years of physical therapy and hundreds of dollars in co-pays, nothing seemed to help. Doctors told me that there was nothing that they could do and that it was just a product of getting older. So, I tried to live with it for another year, but the pain continued and progressed. I finally went to my friend's husband, a chiropractor. It turned out that I was 8 lbs. heavier on one side and completely twisted. The back pain was traveling to my knee, my arm, and my neck and I was wearing a back brace every day. I could hardly lift a dish out of the sink. Despite the weekly trips to the chiropractor, I just couldn't get beyond the pain.

As I prayed, listening to the healing CD and hearing God's promises, I was in so much pain that I cried out to Him that I didn't know what to do; it was getting worse. In the CD, I heard "I will heal you – and I will cure you says the Lord" and I started saying out loud "You said You would heal me and cure me." I didn't know what I was doing, but through the pain and tears, I just said it.

The next morning, it was incredibly cold and icy, and I dreaded the drive into work and the inevitable back pain. I stopped at the bottom of my street, looked left and right for traffic and noticed that my neck didn't feel stiff. Hmm...strange. I got to work and felt okay, so I called and cancelled my appointment. I cancelled the next appointment and have never had to go back! I was completely healed. Completely even, no longer twisted or heavier on one side.

From that day forward, I learned and truly believe that every promise is real, and He hears us. Even if you don't have someone to pray with you – the Holy Spirit will stand in witness, making it two or more in agreement. When you remind Him that He said it, He will watch over His word to perform it. *Jeremiah 1:12 "The Lord tells us that He watches over His word to perform it."*

I learned that you have to speak the words out of your mouth because God is Spirit, and when you speak His words (scripture) out of your mouth and into the atmosphere, He will watch over that word and perform it. It won't come back void, it will accomplish what He intended it to. *Isaiah 55:11 "So shall my word that goes forth out of my mouth it shall not return void, but it shall accomplish that which I please and it will prosper." 2 Corinthians 1:20 "For all promises of God are yes and in Him Amen."* That day, my faith increased, and nothing can ever change that. We must learn to pray using His promises, say them out loud and He promises to be faithful to answer. There is a promise for every circumstance.

Because of that miracle, I really came to know that He is faithful to His promise and that He heard and healed me. When I look back at my life, I know that none of it was wasted. Every person that touched my life – good and bad – shaped me into who I am. Everything that God did, made me love Him more. He was always there; He had always been there answering my prayers, every step of the way.

It was the following Easter that I once again prayed for Shane. When I left him, I had walked away with no closure. I had heard that Janie had somehow convinced him that I was the crazy one. Miriam had stopped over for Easter and he happened to call her to wish her a happy holiday. He asked to speak with me as well, and we talked for a short while. We talked about the happy moments – that's what I wanted, peace with the situation. Of course, I wanted him sober, but my prayer was just to have peace with it and I finally got that.

The following winter the restaurant sank like the Titanic and closed. I have no idea what's happened to either of them. Shane was weak, he couldn't separate from people, places and things and wouldn't try to get help. By not finding the strength to change, the enemy devoured him, and he fell into Satan's trap and he lost it all.

CHAPTER 17
A PRODIGAL WILD CHILD STARTS HEADING BACK HOME

"So he got up and went to his father, but while he was still a long way off, his father saw him and was filled with compassion for him; he ran to his son, threw his arms around him and kissed him. "The son said to him, 'Father, I have sinned against heaven and against you. I am no longer worthy to be called your son.' "But the father said to his servants, 'Quick! Bring the best robe and put it on him. Put a ring on his finger and sandals on his feet. Bring the fattened calf and kill it. Let's have a feast and celebrate. For this son of mine was dead and is alive again; he was lost and is found.' So they began to celebrate." Luke 15: 20-2, NIV

Whatever it is that creates the distance between you and God, when you realize that you've allowed it to happen, you have to fight the demons that pulled you away – vanity, drugs, alcohol, money, sex, good times, or relationships. The darker side of life had slowly crept in over the last sixteen years. Thankfully, I wasn't so far gone that I couldn't recognize where I was. I knew that I had a life to live, but I knew I had to bring it back to God.

There are blessings all around us; we just have to embrace and accept them rather than allow the enemy to steal them. When you've done all that you can or are able to, and still don't know what to do or how to get through things, you just have to bring it back to God.

Opportunities to give up, give in, or allow one to control,

even destroy me, had confronted me my entire life. But, God's grace kept good people in my life to counteract the bad, and He continuously gave me the best friends in the world. I know sometimes people say things like "I don't know what I would do without you." But, I really am one of those people that has just been blessed with the most amazing friends who continue to love me through my crazy, silly adventures. They love me when I do stupid things, make mistakes, or hang on to a bad relationship a lot longer than I should! They've supported me through the hardest times and have been with me during the joyful ones.

He gave me Miriam, a strong Christian woman who remained beside me as a reminder of the love and the power of Jesus and God. She helped me when my relationship with Shane was pulling me down and stood by me when I realized that I had to walk away to save myself.

One of my dearest, truest friends, the wonderful Laly, is, and continues to be, a blessing in so many ways. We met in 2000, in a disconnected way. We didn't go to school together or work together; no common stomping grounds. Nothing that would have made our paths cross. One day after work, I had stopped in Elmsford to get my nails done and sat next to a very chatty lady named Gail. She was getting her nails done with Christmas trees and snowflakes; very festive for the holidays. I couldn't help but talk with her. When she left, she said "Keep in touch honey." So, we did; and every couple of weeks or so she would invite me over.

Often, when someone extends an invite to go out after work, or come over for a party, or just a cup of coffee, we don't

128

take them up on it and we end up missing out on possible work or long-time friendships. Friendship requires you to make the effort to show up when people invite you; or for you to extend an invite.

Gail called one Friday in the summer to say that she was having a couple of girlfriends over and invited me to stop by for a BBQ. Getting an invite to go somewhere with people you don't know can be intimidating. You can feel like a stranger and worry if they will accept you or if you will fit in. I've never been shy, guess you figured that out by now! So, I went.

Laly was one of her friends. We struck up a great conversation and found that we both loved to do things. I remember telling her that I loved shows, plays, street fairs, and music; shopping, dancing, you name it, I'm pretty much up for anything. She said, "Me too!" Then she took the opportunity and invited me to meet her for lunch at the mall. We talked about everything; our families, kids and moms; our lives, and we've kept our relationship going all these years.

We went everywhere! Everywhere! Our kids became friends, our friends became friends. A 'chance' meeting opened up both of our worlds to so many wonderful people and times. I recently became friends with Joan, and now she's friends with Laly, as well as our other friends. I'm glad that she accepted my invitation, because she's a beautiful person and a great addition to our lives. Tonight, while I'm working on this book, she's hanging out with Laly, and for a moment I felt like I was missing out on something – but only for a moment – Emel threw a couch pillow at me to get me back on track and off the text messages! I'm happy that everyone's caring and loving toward one another. That's the concept of Jesus too; He loves all of us and we are all connected through Him.

Family in His eyes are not just our biological family. There's brotherly and sisterly, love; we're all brothers and sisters; we are God's children. I love people in my life, the way He does; it makes me happy to have those people in a relationship with me, but I love when they love one another too. When I see that, I sit back and just soak it in. We're a family of friends who chose each other; each different in our own way and different within the various parts of our lives; yet, each one is loving and accepting, of the other. A true family, we give each other advice; sometimes we take it, sometimes we don't; yet we remain there for one another.

That doesn't mean I have to have someone with me all the time, I like my alone time as well, but during the hardest times in my life, there's always been someone there for me. When you put yourself out there and help others, it comes back to you.

"Em, you love to write, think deep, question and research things. You're spiritual, strong, and always there for your family and friends. When life gets hard, you keep it to yourself. But, I can get it out of you and we know that we have each other to talk with, pray with, cry, laugh and dance with."

"The dancing would be Dionne."

"Yeah, Di's just pure sunshine; bright, cheerful, and a great listener. I'm so thankful to even know the people in my life and have such a deep love for their friendship. Nancy, Dionne and I call our-selves the Three Musketeers."

One Saturday night a few years ago, they wanted to go out to see the Short Bus Band in South Norwalk "SoNo." Great little area, with lots of craft shops, restaurants, bars and bands. Still traumatized from the relationship with Shane, the restaurant bar scene scared me, and I physically trembled in that environment. But Dionne insisted "Jac, come on, are you kidding me, you're going to let this keep you from going out? He's a knucklehead – a bumbling fool!" I loved being with them and realized that isolating myself wasn't the right thing to do. Why should I stay home alone because of someone else's failures?

The Short Bus Band drew a crowd and we danced all night. It got so crowded that we ended up dancing outside in the rain! There was a cute guy, Paul who joined us; we had a blast! At the end of the night he asked if we could stay in touch; I was feeling great, so I said sure. We went to dinner the following week, and found that we had similar work backgrounds, and break up stories. He had been in a toxic relationship and started questioning his faith but met a waitress that told him about a church that she attended. Though he was a skeptic when it came to religion, he needed to find solace and started attending Stanwich Congregational Church in Greenwich. He said that the Sunday evening service was done with alternative worship music and he really enjoyed going there and invited me to come. It sounded comforting, so I took him up on the offer and decided to go the following Sunday.

I had taken my relationship with Shane as far as I could and accepted that I just couldn't do anymore for him, I needed to get back to God for my own self. Through this new-found friendship, I found my new church; Paul was a set-up by God! He was a "random" person that I met dancing one night; cute enough to go to dinner with, but our political views were a deal breaker. But that was God putting the right person, for the right reason in my life at that moment. Not to give me a romantic relationship, but to get me back to church, back to Him.

Stanwich Congressional is one of the most beautiful places; so elegant and sound. The people are warm, the worship updated, the voices like angels. I felt such heartache over the situation I left behind with Shane. I cared about him, but there was nothing I could do except pray; it weighed heavily on my heart. Miriam decided to go with me to Stanwich. It was about a 45-minute ride each way, but we knew that we needed to be there. The Evening Service was called "Evensong."

After each service they had a wonderful buffet dinner and round tables were set up for fellowship. There was plenty to get involved with; missions, sports, Bible studies, so many activities and all well done. Miriam and I are both social, so we joined right in. I was starting to notice that the congregation really seemed to know and talk about the Bible. I knew the gospel and Jesus, but I didn't know much of the Old Testament, you know, other than the Ten Commandments, Noah's Ark, and watching the story of Moses on T.V. It frightened me when I learned at Saint Anthony's that God turned Lot's wife into a pillar of salt for turning back at Sodom. That's what the fear of God meant to me and I didn't really understand Him because of that, so I always felt like I had to do everything right or else.

I wanted to converse more with the new people I was meeting, I just didn't know where to start. Where was the begi-

-nning? Genesis? I know God created the world in seven days, but that was all I knew as the beginning. I started waking up in the mornings thinking about where the beginning was.

During the service, the Word was always projected with white letters on a white candle lit wall; very serene and beautiful. The Senior Pastor was powerfully anointed in heart and intellect. The church was calm and still, the Holy Spirit always present, and there it was - white letters projected on the wall illuminated by candlelight. *John 1: 1-3: "In the beginning was the "WORD" and the word was with God and the word was God. He was with God in the Beginning." Verse 14, "The WORD became flesh and made his dwelling with us."*

The Pastor started talking about the Greek word, "Debar" meaning Divine Word – prophecy, true, the climax of the incarnation of Jesus. Boom! Like dynamite it hit me! Jesus was the Word who manifest into flesh. He is God and the Word always existed. There really was no beginning in the "Greek" original writing of the Bible because the Word has always been alive. It's Him talking. He never lies. I was never afraid of Jesus, so that took away my fear of God. In fact, I really wanted to know more, so I went back to the beginning of the book and started in Genesis and I read; and I read; and I read; and read some more.

My brother had given me my mother's Bible, and I had been keeping it in a drawer. I gently turned the pages where she had marked with all different color highlighters. At that moment, I knew she knew that what I was relearning, were the things that she had taught me. Things I already knew, but there was so much more to know. I couldn't get enough. I started printing out books at a time, reading them one by one, marking them up myself; looking up things I didn't know or understand; digging deeper and deeper. I needed to learn everything! I even got a filing cabinet to keep every copy as I studied them. There is no way you can ever get bored, there's just so much wisdom in the Bible; history, math, psychology, war, science, order, protection, guidance, it's perfect, flawless. It is the best love story ever written. I was so incredibly awed by God! I loved the Old Testament and was bursting to share everything with Miriam, the new church friends I was making, and my mom – oh my mom, if only she were here.

*She was mom, she protected us, taught us, reasoned
with us. I give her so much credit for who I am.*

CHAPTER 18
LOSING MY MOTHER

"Whoever believes in Jesus shall have eternal life with Him. Whoever believes in Him should not perish but have eternal life. For God so loved the world that He gave His only begotten Son, that whoever believes in Him should not perish but have everlasting life…Jesus prepares a dwelling place in Heaven for those who believe in Him."
John 3:15-17, NIV

"My Father's house has many rooms; if that were not so, would I have told you that I am going there to prepare a place for you?" John 14:2 ESV

When I was 5, I used to walk home from kindergarten for lunch. My mother would pretend not to see me and say "Oh, where's the baby?" then "There's my girl!" It was so special. She would make me a hot lunch and set it up on a small wooden table and chair set. I especially liked Campbell's chicken noodle soup on winter days.

Together we would watch Kimba the White Lion, my favorite cartoon. I can still hear the theme song as the smiling little white lion appeared to be running toward the screen, while the other jungle animals that followed him sang, "Kimba, Kimba, Kimba the White Lion was his name. When we get in trouble and we're in a fight, who's the one who just won't turn and run? Who believes in doing good and doing right? Kimba the white lion is the one!" I'd sing along everyday waiting for his adventure to start.

She was diagnosed with cancer a few years ago, and as

she got closer to the end, it helped that we were a family of believers. She and I wanted to make a pact. You know the one - if it's possible from heaven to give a sign. It's the kind of thing that runs through your mind, but we never had the chance to say exactly what that sign would be. I was so focused on life and raising my son. She watched him when I was trying to get on my feet. He was special to my mother; he was her hero and he adored her.

Several months after she passed, my sister told me that she received a package from Mom to Beau – but we didn't know how or why it arrived so long after she was gone. He opened the brown parcel taped box. It was a white lion. But how? We had never agreed to anything, but that's what she sent. Was the gift a sign to me, it came to us in such a strange way. Even with the greatest of faith and knowing that our loved ones are home with our Lord in a far better place; occurrences like this bring us extraordinary awareness and comfort.

My mother raised three good kids, she really shared her heart and her love of Jesus with us. In a lot of ways, she developed my relationship with Him. She reasoned with us. Many of her qualities are mine as well. Keeping your word, never letting others down. She was reliable, but she also knew how to be private and would keep your words in confidence, it never went beyond her. She loved life and she lived it! Things weren't always neat and orderly, rarely organized or structured. That pretty much skipped a generation with me! She didn't sweat the details - she wasn't materialistic. Her passion was love, life, her family and she had a strong conviction, a deeply rooted love in Christ. She was Mrs. C.; she was the Brownie leader, Girl Scout leader, she loved kids. She had three of us, but we were each allowed to take two friends with us anywhere we went – camp mom without the camp! She took us to the City, The Statue of Liberty, museums, the park; she rolled down hills with us, took us ice skating on a frozen lake, taught us to swim in the summer, you name it, she was one of us. But, she was mom, she protected us, taught us, reasoned with us. I give her so much credit for who I am. Even though there are things about her that I didn't understand growing up, I turned out like her by the grace of God.

"How did she tell you about the cancer?"

"Em, she had such a high tolerance for pain. She was sick once before but remained active. When Beau was four-years old, she was diagnosed with "Guillain-Barre Syndrome," a dormant syndrome we all have that attacks parts of our nervous system; hers activated and caused paralysis."

It was upsetting to hear her say that her hands had no sensation and felt like flippers. She was an artist; she drew and painted, but paralysis kept her from doing anything during that time. Beau has such talent and imagination, I think he's an artist because of her talent and influence. Always content just being by her side, he would make wrestling animal figures out of pipe cleaners, always entertaining her and himself.

With her focus on recovering for Beau, she eventually came out of paralysis. She kept her faith, got her senses back and went right back to painting. But in 1998, renal cell carcinoma, kidney cancer, was discovered at a deadly stage 4. Mom was up on everything; she educated herself on the diagnosis, treatments, the effects of medications, and did her research for the best doctors. She went through surgery, had her kidney removed, but within weeks she was out shoveling snow and ice! Really a true survivor – she had things to do! She went through it, got on with her life and her family. She ate healthy, watched her meds, prayed; walked my Aunt's very large, very active Alaskan Husky, Shadow, in the park.

January 20, 2000, it wasn't unusual for her to be gone for an hour in two feet of snow to walk Shadow. But this night, she was gone a lot longer, it was dark and freezing cold. By some miracle, our neighbor, Raul, went out for a walk that night – why he happened to walk through the park late that night – I have no idea. He found her lying in the snow with Shadow curled around her head. Hypothermia had set in and she had broken her hip in the fall. The hospital x-rays found a very large black spot. We thought it was where her kidney had been removed, but it was around the break in her hip. Bone cancer. The doctors gave her two months to live.

I have to tell you though – that wasn't happening to my mom! She wasn't having it! Most people would have given up and not gone through with the treatment. As long as she could move her little toe, she was going to make it! Despite the prognosis, she had hip surgery. Beau and I were with her through every surgery and visited her every day. She was completely wrapped up like a mummy at times, with blinking lights and things that circulated and hummed around her hospital room. She wanted to know if I had brought her sneakers! Really? In her mind, she was ready to get up and walk out. She just wanted to walk down the hallway; but the doctors remained strict.

A titanium rod was put in her leg during the hip replace-

-ment procedure. After the surgery, she was transferred to a great rehab center in White Plains. Mom motivated everyone right from her wheelchair. Though she was given two months, while others faced longer or normal lives and complained of their knee replacement surgeries, this pain or that ache; she ignored it and was thankful for everything. She knew the prognosis but denied the outcome. As a family, we really tried to do all the right things; we visited, played Scrabble, ate dinner with her and talked about the day.

She fought through the chemo attacking the aggressive cancer raging through her body. Unfortunately, she was transferred from rehab right back into the next hospital and she hated it. She told us that she was left alone on a gurney in the hallway alone way too long and insisted on going to chemo as an out-patient; she wanted to be in her own home. It was incredibly difficult, but we did it. Families keep making choices. For us, it was the right thing to do.

We all made sacrifices, but not anywhere near what my mother did. My sister was our saving grace. She gave up a potential career to be a lawyer and went to nursing school so that she could care for our mother. She really took amazing care of her, got her to appointments, watched and measured medications, put the wheelchair in and out of the car and stayed on top of everything. Mom loved a day bed that I had, and since she could no longer climb stairs, we set it up in our first-floor dining room with a fresh new comforter and linens. It was her first day home since the fall in the park. She had endured multiple surgeries, hospitals, a hip replacement, rehab,more hospitals and was finally back in the comfort of her own home to rest and sleep.

Dad was never very domesticated, but he tried to take care of the house and chores. He had smoked most of his life and eventually quit, but during my mom's illness, he was still chain smoking. One afternoon, he was on the second floor, gathering laundry and thought he had put his cigarette out completely before he emptied the ashtray into the trash can, but it was still hot. He went outside and around the house, lifted the ground level doors and went down to the cellar to start the washer. He had no idea that the second floor had caught on fire and was burning, while my mother slept on the first floor in the daybed.

Two Spanish men in sharp crisp suits were walking by on this freezing day. They must have seen the smoke, used their cell phone to call 911 and the fire department. They ran into the house and rescued my mom. My dad went back into the house, not even realizing what was happening, until he felt the heat burning the bottom of his feet; he couldn't go any further into the house. He ended up with second degree burns on both feet. When he ran back outside, he found that the two men had carried Mom out.

The fire department arrived, and when my parents turned to thank the two strangers, they were gone without a trace. Coincidence? Could it be that two Spanish men in crisp impeccable suits on a cold winter day, wearing no coats, just happened to be walking by my parent's house? They pulled her out of a burning home, then disappeared without a trace, not even to hear a thank you? Were they angels? Yes. Absolutely Yes!

An angel can appear as a person – just like the two strang

-ers that arrived and rescued my mom. I've always wondered if my mother called for her angels or if they simply were already there, anticipating what could have been a tragedy.

During her days of cancer, my mom really felt that after a year she was going to be cured. For us, as a family going through it, we tried to be strong for and with her. It was very draining, but to watch someone you love suffering was even harder. It was very difficult to get her everywhere she needed to be, while maintaining our own lives.

As a single parent, it wasn't always easy for me to get off work, visit or help; and to have my little boy in waiting rooms, a part of this, and watching him grow up under the emotional strain was very difficult. I would get so tired that I couldn't even think straight. It's not like a cold or passing bug, it's a disease and you never know when it's going to end or where it will lead.

During one of her surgeries, she was at New York Hospital for Special Services, in Manhattan. Despite the blizzards and snow storms that seemed to come one after the other that year, my father and I drove back and forth every single day to see her. It was expensive; medications even more expensive; switching meds and staying on top of it; finding parking on the street so that we didn't have to pay exorbitant parking fees, but we managed through it.

Dad worked on the west side of Manhattan and would leave his car parked there and take the bus to the east side to visit Mom. At the end of the night, I would give him a ride back to his car. Once, I repeatedly circled the blocks of Manhattan looking for parking! It was difficult enough on a normal day, but nearly impossible with snow and ice filled streets. I remember finally finding a parking space with scaffolding poles near it. I walked straight, heading in the direction of the hospital, made a left and spent the day with my mother.

It was a frigid night with below zero temperatures and whipping winds. I had no memory on to how to get back to my car. I remembered scaffolding – that was about it!

We walked up and down, in circles around those streets, freezing. With my father saying "Jacquelyn, are these the poles? Are these the poles? How about this one?" No car...no car...no car! We went to the police station thinking that it had been towed or stolen. They put us in a police car and circled us around the blocks until we found my car. It just really goes to show you how out of sorts you can be when you're doing that day after day after day. Trying to keep track of everything and everyone, under such emotional distress. Because you care, you'll do anything.

Weekdays were loaded with appointments, but the family was together for dinner every Sunday; Mom was the glue. Those moments were very precious to us. Every year on my birthday, I had some sort of a theme party; Badda Bing- Badda Boom, The Oscars, Roaring 20's, all different types, even Hunk-A-Mania in my wild child days. I always love that day because I'm surrounded by my friends; each one a part of the person I am today.

During the years that my mother was battling cancer, each year that she was alive on my birthday, was a special gift to me. One year for my theme birthday party, my friends and I piled into a stretch limo on our way to special event. It was March and still cold, but I wore a sequined gold, heavy metal halter top anyway! My hair was in an up-do about 3 feet high – yes it was! I had the chauffer drive by the house, beep the horn and holler for my mom to come out on the porch. Standing up through the sunroof with as many friends as possible in the opening, we waved up at my mom so that she knew I was having a good time and she could be part of the day. I went back the next day to tell her about my night - with my day-old hair still up from all the spray – maybe slightly less than 3 feet by then.

After some time, her cancer had spread, each time requiring yet another surgery. She had lymph nodes removed, and within months part of her stomach. Though she was able to come home, she ended up back in the hospital for something else. When there was a stretch of time where she was home long enough, she'd do things she had no business doing like continuing her regular routine of shopping, buying and returning. Nothing was going to keep her down! She continued with her life of church and visiting friends. It was remarkable how over the course of four years she outlasted the two months she was given. The house continuously got modified, from her regular bed to a hospital bed; the bathroom to a commode; each time, dreading having to be dependent on others. It wasn't her style.

June 2004 my mother's prognosis changed, and she was given only 8 more weeks to live. She announced that she wanted to go on a family cruise, so we took off from New York on the cruise ship named "Miracle" and headed to Orlando and then on to the Bahamas. The family swam with dolphins, went sightseeing and shopping. Mom was determined to get a Gilligan's Island style hat, in yellow.

"Em, my mother was full of life and love; the disease was

taking her life, but she refused to allow it to take her spirit. She was amazing. I don't know if I would have been as strong as she was." As soon as we docked in Orlando, Beau and I took off to Disney's "Island of Adventure." When we returned to the ship, we shared the experiences of the day with my mom and celebrated together.

When we returned home from the cruise, she couldn't walk very much; only from her bed to the commode and back. While she had always been of sound mind, she was starting to have a difficult time remembering what day of the week it was. To help and comfort her, we put up a sign each day next to a large digital clock. She managed to still talk on the phone every day to her friends and kept inviting people over. Sometimes she had no idea how many people were over, and would say "Jacquelyn, would you like some potato salad?" That was my cue to go make potato salad. Of course, I would – just never really knowing how many people were showing up!

No one ever spoke of how she started withering away. Although it became harder with each passing day, we wouldn't show it. Hospice told us what signs to look for when a body starts to shut down. She didn't want to die in the hospital, so we agreed as a family to care for her at home every day until her last day. When someone is dying, you don't want them to leave, yet you don't want them to suffer; and you can't just sit staring at them listening to the clock tick.

"Em, it was Sunday of Labor Day weekend. My father was outside mixing cement to fix a brick wall. I had made chicken cutlets with broccoli rabe over cavatelli, while my brother played his guitar for her, which she loved so much. We didn't know if we should act normal in the room with her or be quiet and softly let her go? We watched her breathing get harder and harder; so deep and fast, until it finally stopped. My brother and I were the only two sitting with her when she passed. Everything had been prearranged; it was time to call the funeral home. The funeral home director arrived at the house, both he and I lifted my mom off the bed and placed her in the body bag. We cared for her body for so long, I couldn't bear for any bones to be broken. We zipped up the bag, took her downstairs on the gurney and into the hearse."

"Jackie, I'm so sorry. I can only imagine how hard that must have been for you. How did you get back to your life after all this?"

"It didn't really hit me until almost a year later. Everyone in my family had someone to lean on. I had my Beau, only 13 years old; and I had to be strong for both of us. You can't get depressed, you can't stay down. You have to keep getting up and realize that there's still a future. You don't stop loving people because they're not physically with you; and you never truly get over their loss. But, you have to keep living and knowing that one day, you will be together again."

God has prepared a place for us; my mom is there with rewards greater than anything here in this short life. Although pain and life may seem long on earth, compared to eternity we're just a blip in time. It really does mean so much to a family when people attend the service for someone they love so much, it's something that you don't forget. They're an extended family that has been woven together by the threads of love. My mom, even throughout her suffering, thanked Jesus every step of the way; she kept her eyes on Him. She thanked Him for getting her through every day, every surgery, every breath, and every moment. She thanked Him for being with her, for her children. She managed to take care of every detail, so that nothing would need to be done after she was gone.

Together with my brother, she had searched for her plot at the cemetery close to home. She told me that there really wasn't much space available, except for an area, high on the hill at the edge of the cemetery where you could hear cars going by on the Parkway. But she said that she didn't mind that, we had always lived on a busy street anyway. She decided that was where she wanted to be. I hadn't had a chance to see the spot until the day of her burial. To my amazement, she was buried in the center of the section that was devoted to infants and toddlers who died at an early age; so significant of her love and dedication to children.

Solid in her convictions and in her relationship with Christ she just believed in Him and the protection of children. She loved, loved, loved both with all of her heart and was always a strong advocate in her own way. I can't express enough to you how deeply she loved Jesus and His children.

Since she was buried so close to home, I'm able to visit there often. Every Labor Day weekend marks an anniversary of another year gone by. The area is always surrounded by balloons, stuffed animals and toys for the children buried around her. I've since learned about those families and how they loved and lost their children, and I tell them that my mom is right inthe middle. I know my Mom is with Jesus and all His little children.

I'm left with her wisdom and all that she taught me; all

those early days of reasoning, and the later days of discussions – all the confidences and the love that we shared. I'm left with no regrets, only beautiful memories and a love that can never die.

I am so very proud of my family and the way that we all loved her. I'm thankful to my brother and his wife, a true sister. On days when the fever ran so high, she commuted from Brooklyn and was there with cold compresses and to talk with my mom, while bringing her fever down. My brother-in-law and my sister moved into my Grandmother's old apartment downstairs after they got married. He was always there to help, usually wearing a tie-dyed t-shirt, Star Wars or something interesting and had plenty of sci-fi stories to tell her. I'm not too sure she understood all the sci-fi adventures, but he was lots of fun and extremely humorous; she loved him so much.

I think the greatest thanks goes to my sister who had it the hardest and yet never wanted to hear 'thank you.' She believed that it was simply what you do. But in my heart, I can't thank her enough for the sacrifices she made in switching careers and living in the house for years. She and her husband could have moved out and been on their own, but they stayed. They stayed through every appointment, every medication Beau was always there by her side. Those childhood years were ones that he should have been playing with friends, but he was with her every week and every hospital visit. She loved him the most. It wasn't easy for him to watch her go through everything, but he was so sweet and so strong; so much more than just my little boy. When you're going through something like this, you keep on doing what needs to be done; and when it stops... it all stops, and the world feels very still.

My son is, and always will be, the most important person in my life. If he should ever say, "Carry You," I'll be right by his side to do just that!

CHAPTER 19
OUR CHILDREN

"Behold, children are a heritage from the Lord, the fruit of the womb, a reward." Psalms 127:30, NIV

It's been over twenty-four years since my divorce. I had great people in my life, and some not so great people crossed my path as well. It hasn't exactly been easy street for me, where things simply fell into place. I had to work hard and hold on as tight as I could to my faith, even when I questioned why God let things happen. But, whatever it was that I was going through and experiencing, my son was always the most important person in my world.

"Jackie, you cracked me up when we first met. You two were always going somewhere, doing something. Heavy metal rock concerts, deep sea fishing! I've always been amazed at your dedication to make sure you did the things he liked."

"I really always liked to do things together and to experience all that life has to offer. I wanted my house to be in order, then we'd go do something. He really loved music – still does, so concerts were huge for us. The genre never mattered to me as long as we went together, and it made him happy."

Don't think that my father's eccentricity didn't rub off on my parenting skills! One year, Beau was in summer camp and had a part in a play. The story involved a ghost, a werewolf, a monster and this little girl that was looking to make friends. The little girl knocked on their doors. Beau's line was really just a 'Owwooooo" the cutest little howl, and of course I wanted to go see it. I was working at a very strict company at the time and we weren't really supposed to go out to lunch or leave our desk, but I was determined to take the half hour ride to get there and the half hour back. Mom had been diagnosed with cancer back then, but she was determined to go too. I made it to the camp and got to my seat, all ready to watch the play...and it was over! Because, I'm usually late to everything! I told the counselor that I had come all this way and pleaded with her to have the kids do it again! Beau was embarrassed, and when it came time for his howl, he wouldn't howl.

I loved seeing him in his element, and always wanted to be in the first row, I was so proud of him. Despite my always wanting to be at everything he did, whether it was a school concert, or play, he didn't always appreciate my enthusiasm. Especially when he was on the wrestling team, and I was practically on the mat next to him. I was afraid Godzilla was going to twist my kid into a knot and I would scream "Pin him Beau! Pin him!" His friends would smile and say, 'Beau your Mom's here." His response, "She could be in Giant's stadium, and you'd know my Mom was here."

He spent hours in his room, pulling up music tabs on his computer and stringing his guitar. He wasn't interested in the beach or the pool anymore and just wanted to focus on drawing, writing, and playing his guitar. Our door was always open, so his closest friends felt comfortable coming over at random times and were happy being in the house creating. They were out of trouble and I liked that I knew where they were; they were fun to have around; messy, very messy, but fun.

Together, they assembled their first high school band, Odyssey. Beau played bass, sang, wrote the lyrics and composed and co-composed the music with his friend Max, who played guitar. Max's girlfriend was their vocalist, they had a drummer and a lead guitarist, Kenny. All three boys were like sons to me. They wrestled in High School; watched extreme fighting, loved the WWE; created and filmed their own stunts, wrote music for it; and added the credits at the end.

Beau began cartooning, writing comic strips, sculpting and animating. His drawings were outstanding, and he and Max started a comic strip called Gomez Studios. It was about a newt named Gomez who got caught up in a science experiment and turned into a super hero, with allies, villains and political characters. Later he started sculpting them and creating animation; together with Max and their friend Kyle, they started filming and writing more episodes. It was amazing, yet, Beau never thought anything of it. To him everything was just a doodle. His school thought differently; he was winning art awards.

One Christmas, he wanted to go to the Clause Fest concert. I figured it would be something cool to do together, so I got the tickets. Whoa! It was a whole lot of different from the R&B I listened too. It was Korn, Velvet Revolver, Papa Roach and six other bands that I didn't know. Giant's stadium was packed!! The bass of the music was so loud that it pounded in my chest as I watched hundreds of Santa Clauses being thrown around in the mosh pit. I looked over at Beau and he was rocking out. I thought to myself, the kid is so cool!!!!!

The energy of the concert and the music pumping, my son just came alive! It was so amazing to see how my little boy had grown from an infant, to a toddler, and now a young teen. He could hang out and really rocked out, head whipping, and he knew every word to every song. On the ride home, he asked for an electric guitar.

For his 16th birthday I got him a bass guitar. When he plugged it in and played, I cried – not because of the decibels and the walls vibrating, but because it was amazing, like someone on America's Got Talent, where your jaw drops from the unexpected gifted talent. He could play, I mean really play. Again, he didn't think much of it. It wasn't that he was even trying to be humble, he just didn't think anything he did was extraordinary.

Once I saw how much he loved the experience and the music, whenever he wanted to go see a band, we'd go. The days of going to the circus or the zoo, turned into rock and heavy metal concerts. It opened me up to a whole other realm of genres and crazy, head banging, loud, pyro music, but I enjoyed my journey and spending time with him.

When people at work asked what I did over the weekend, I'd tell them that I went with my son to this concert or that concert. They'd ask, "Does he know how cool you are?" I would just smile and respond, "No, I doubt it." I'm the only mom he had and there weren't any other parents for him to compare me to. I tried to always do the things he was interested in; I didn't judge.

For his 21st birthday, he wanted to see the Big Four at the new Yankee Stadium. Wow! He wanted me to go with him for his 21st Birthday! Of course, I agreed, and we took two of his friends. Thousands of people rocked out to 10 hours of AC/DC,

Slayer, Megadeath and Anthrax. He shared with me how all four connected; he knew every single band, who played what, who changed, and the history of each. There's a mutual respect between the bands and the fans; a respect for one another and the music they share, which is pretty cool.

My co-workers couldn't believe that I sat through 10 hours of that concert! But, I loved seeing my son happy, and in his element – and I liked some of the music as well. Music is a release – it can release anger, frustration, solitude; it can bring peace, joy and comfort; it can bring resolution to broken hearts, lives.

There were times when he brought friends and we would fit as many as we could legally into my car. Once, we drove with Max through a hurricane, then sat in seats with garbage bags over us with the rain pouring down, just so they could see Stain and Janes Addiction. Another time, we went out to the Hamptons to see Dream Theatre. We've seen Linkin Park, Aerosmith, Motley Crew, Joe Satriani; so many others, that I can't begin to list them all, or the places we've traveled to see them.

My son still loves to go to concerts, and the cool thing is, he still asks me if I want to come. He's a bassist, guitarist, writer and artist. When he writes and arranges his own music, he'll often share it with me. I love that time with him and listening to what he's created. I love what he does, even if it's not my style, I can see and experience the talent that he's been given. His interests became my interests and I encouraged them all. He learns everything so easily and has a super creative mind.

Our lives and choices effect our children; I did my best to protect and love him and put him above all others – including myself. When he really got out there with his band, I recognized that look of comfort that a child gets knowing that their mother or father was there to support and cheer them on. At least I'd like to believe that we had that connection and he loved me being there. That alone means so much to me. I've always told him that whatever he wanted to do and whatever he wanted to become, that I would walk by his side, even if his choices weren't ones that I agreed with; or the life that I wanted for him, he was still his own person and I would always stand by him.

As much as we did a lot of things together, and I love him in some ways like a little brother, or as my best friend, I always loved him as my son. When he questioned or challenged why he had to do something my way, I would remind him that I was still the parent.

We often ask God why, and He says "Because, I'm your parent." When we don't listen, and something goes wrong, He told us so. I have to say that Beau always respected me, and I always respected him. Growing up, I allowed him to have long hair, or an earring; listen to his style of music – unless it was way too dark – then I verbalized that I didn't like it, and in some cases, just out right forbid it. But, other things were a discussion. More than anything, I wanted my son to be safe, and I wanted him to be with me forever. But I also had to be careful and respectful, and let him learn his way the way my parents had allowed me to. Beau is a good person, loyal, reliable and a hard worker. He's an absolute love. He always knew that he could come to me and talk to me about anything; God gave me the strength and wisdom to give him real honest answers and advice. I will never stop praying for him and will never stop believing that he will soar in this life through his amazing talents. I trust God; Beau is His son first and I'm his mother whom God trusted with his life. God is good, this I know. There is a plan for his life, and I'm so thankful that we remain close, and trust that we always will.

In many ways I've carried my son through his whole life; through his struggles and challenges, and through his victories. So often, I ask God to give me the strength to continue to carry him through life no matter what it takes. He's no longer the little boy that I can pick up and carry, but we've been by each other's side through hard times; and we will always be by each other's side for years to come. As a loving mother, I will always be there to carry him through whatever comes his way; I know he will always be there to do the same for me.

That's the way God loves us too. He really wants the best for us, but He allows us to take our own path and He stands beside us. I love my son, no matter what decisions he makes in his life. I love what he shares with me and I love the person he is. Though he and I have very different views on most things, we meet at a point of respect, compassion and real love.

CHAPTER 20
FORGIVENESS

"And be kind to one another, tenderhearted, forgiving one another, even as God in Christ forgave you."
Ephesians 4:32
"Forgiveness does not excuse bad behavior. Forgiveness prevents the bad behavior of others from destroying your heart." —Author Unknown.

Throughout my life, I have had to face situations that required forgiveness in one way or another, whether it was for someone that directly hurt me, or someone that indirectly caused me pain. The greater the relationship, the deeper the pain and anger, and when betrayal creeps in, it can be so very hard to forgive. Resentment can grow, especially when others say that you need to forgive to move on. But, that really is the truth; the way to freedom and peace is through forgiveness. It has nothing to do with feelings; it's a choice we can exercise so that we can move forward in our own lives.

We've all heard that time heals all wounds; in time we'll get over the pain enough to be able to forgive and move on; or that we need to forgive and forget. Forgiveness becomes con-fused with "it's better now and you can come back into my life." But none of this is true. None of this is what forgiveness means at all. It's not time that heals, its sincere forgiveness that heals us. Forgiveness is really all about RELEASE. That's it. All you have to do is release the person and hand their fate over to God, and let God deal with that person's heart.

There is no reason to monitor the ones who have hurt you or wish them harm; stalk them on social media; or feel upset, even jealous that they seem to be happier than you are. They are still who they are, and you have released yourself from their grasp. There is a better plan in your future that God prepared for you; don't let the past hold you back; forgive and release.

I forgave Joe a very long time ago and was able to move on with my life. He remains abusive, bitter, and without knowing God, he remains himself. When I realized that God forgave me for my past sins, and even the sins that I will commit in my future, I learned what true forgiveness meant. No one is without sin and it's impossible to go through life without being offended. We will either sin against others or they will sin against us. These are stumbling blocks that we have to experience in order to grow, while we learn to trust in God.

As Christians we're viewed as having to like everyone, but we don't; we can't. It would be nice to be able to, but not very realistic to think that we have to like people who are immoral or of ill intent. So, what do we do? We have to release them and turn their outcome over to God. That's it. Don't judge them and don't attach to them. Be smart enough to navigate around those who will only bring you down; those who will constantly relive the damage that hurt you and bring it back into your heart and mind; those who will only cause more pain, anger or resentment. If you can, "let go and let God," then you can begin the journey to freedom.

Now, that doesn't mean that you will instantly be okay when you forgive someone. Forgiveness may become repetitive, you may have to forgive every day or every month, until you truly make peace with it and fully accept that you've for-given them. Whatever happened to cause the pain is real, and it's not fine. The hurt may still be there, but you have to release it and turn it over to God; and if you feel the pain creep back in, bring it right back to God.

Jesus said to His disciples in *Luke 17:1 "Offenses will certainly come, but woe to the one they come through!" Romans 12:19 says never to take revenge, but leave room for God's wrath, for it is written, "I will take revenge; I will pay them back, says the LORD."* God is a just God. He is the ulti-mate judge and He will settle your case; you don't need to seek revenge or manipulate the outcome.

Jesus wants us to surrender our anger and pain to Him. He forgave us, and He asks that we forgive others by releasing it over to Him. Ideally, the best forgiveness could be to apolo-gize and reconcile a broken relationship, if that relationship is healthy. However, so often, we have a very hard time because we gave our heart to something or someone that started out good, but our heart or faith was broken. We tend to rest in what felt right in the beginning and hope it returns even after being hurt or abused. When we forgive others, we are doing it for ourselves; it allows the restoration of our spirit with Jesus. We are created to have a purposeful life, not one of bondage.

When we talk about forgiving others, remember that we need to forgive ourselves as well. While I've forgiven those who have hurt me, I too have asked for forgiveness from those I have hurt unintentionally. We're not perfect. I'm not perfect. I'm human and have weaknesses and need direction. Sometimes, I don't want to change the areas that I'm vulnerable in. But, a

159

humble spirit brings strength in admitting that we are all sinners and we are all works in progress.Sometimes, just in the process of living our own lives, we hurt the ones we love the most. I truly believe that when love is genuine, and forgiveness is sincere, it will heal any situation. Not forgiving will have the opposite effect. Pride and arrogance are two traits from the enemy and are behaviors that are not trophies to be proud of *"... pride goes before destruction and arrogance before the fall" Proverbs 16:18.*

Pride caused Lucifer, the most beautiful of all the angels, to think he was better than God himself. In wanting control, he caused eternal separation from love; from God. When pride and arrogance are used to bully or control others, to appear in the right long enough, relationships that once meant so much are lost. After pride, the fall begins; resentment seeps in; family disputes start, there are break-ups, separations, divorces and gossip. We have the power to choose to be humble enough to say that we are sorry. It's not such a tough a pill to swallow and it makes a tremendous difference in the lives of those we care about, as well as our own lives.

Whether or not we ever get an apology from someone who's offended us, or we have tried to apologize to someone who won't forgive us, we can still make the decision to forgive and release. *"If we confess our sins, He is faithful and just to forgive us our sins and to cleanse us from all unrighteousness" 1 John 1:19.*

The choice is ours. If our prayers aren't being answered, perhaps it's because somewhere in our heart we haven't fully forgiven someone, and the anger still lingers. If you know what's holding you back, ask God to help you through it;

if you don't know, then ask Him to reveal what is preventing your blessings from coming through. Forgiving is not always easy, and it may take repetitive efforts, but it is truly possible.

CHAPTER 21
CALLED BY GOD

"The spirit of the sovereign Lord is on me, because the Lord has anointed me to proclaim good news to the poor. He has sent me to bind up the broken hearted, to proclaim freedom for the captives and release from darkness for the prisoners." Isaiah 61:1, NIV

"At what point did you decide you wanted to become a minister?"

"I didn't. It was a calling that happened in March 2011."

"How did you know?"

"Em, when God speaks to you, there's no denying His Word."

The year before, I had met Jared at my church, Stanwich Congregational. He owned a shop in my town and was an amazing extreme sportsman. We spent the spring and summer riding miles of seemingly endless bike trails, hiking, rock-climbing and kayaking. We both had a heart for missions, and often did midnight runs to destitute sections of Manhattan, delivering clothes, coats and meals to the homeless. Several months later we spoke to the Senior Pastor about Christian dating.

Many weekends were spent with his family at their beach house on the Jersey Shore or with my friends and family. He was a stellar boyfriend for the first seven months while we were being mentored by the Pastor. I thought God had finally comforted me by giving me a good Christian man; one that felt safe and trustworthy. I had a lot of hope that he would mature and understand the love of Christ, however, he was an infant Christian. Though he had recently accepted Jesus, he hadn't really surrendered to Christ, he was still blaming others for his problems and not accepting any of his own weaknesses or issues. Our relationship turned out to be the next leg of my journey.

Becoming a Christian isn't easy. Christian maturity requires you to rid yourself of the wrongful desires of the flesh and work towards becoming more in the image of Christ. If we were to compare heaven to a gym - I know that sounds strange but go with me for a minute. Accepting Jesus gives you access to salvation in heaven; like having a membership gives you access to a gym. When you go to the gym, you have to identify your physical flaws and use the right machines to get rid of them. Spiritual maturity works the same way – you have to be honest with yourself and identify your character flaws, you must apply God's direction to mature. Spiritual changes, like physical ones, require discipline to see results.

Yes, you can accept Jesus into your life, but, that's not enough, you have to work and learn to apply the word and directions of the Bible to your life. It's hard to surrender yourself to become more like Christ. Jared didn't surrender himself, he was going to church, like going to the gym, but not using the machines. He wasn't using the word of God to change. So, then what was the purpose of going to church? He didn't work out things through God – he didn't mature.

Passive-aggressive patterns started becoming more apparent in his behavior. He started growing odd shaped beards and mutton chops and when I asked him to shave them off, he said that he would. Instead, weeks went by and they became so distorted and hideous that it forced me to ask him again. He was intentionally using his passive-aggressive behavior to create tension between us. It was as if he was trying to piss me off, and he was! He began disrespecting my home by leaving his things everywhere; dirty clothes and gym bag on the white carpet. That beard really aggravated me to no end! I hated looking at him or being seen with him looking that way, so I began to distance myself. He finally shaved it off!

Shortly after that, in November, he, along with other church members went on a mission trip to Haiti to help rebuild after a hurricane. When they returned several weeks later, I picked them up from the airport and drove them back to the church. Everyone got into their cars and took off; I was happy to finally be alone with him again and really wanted to hear about his experience. Driving home, he abruptly started yelling at me. I couldn't believe it! His words were a blow by blow punch to my heart.

Over the last few weeks, he had internalized his anger and suddenly exploded with rage, claiming that I had tricked him and manipulated him into shaving. Every time I tried to speak, he would tell me that he would let me know when I could talk! I sat there stunned, listening to him, not knowing if I should yell or cry – instead, I remained silenced.

Growing up, his mother had been controlling, so anytime a woman tried to say something that came across as correcting him, he didn't know how to properly communicate and would react in a spiteful way. This wasn't the first time he had yelled at me; but I noticed that once he started, he was stuck on a track that he couldn't switch off and raged on relentlessly.

When we finally got him home, he asked me to come in, but I just couldn't bring myself to even get out of the car. It would have been like walking into the lion's den. He wasn't going to let up. Driving away, my heart raced and took my breath away. How could someone come back from a heartfelt mission helping people and be this monstrous? As I turned down the street to go home, he pulled alongside me in his truck, I thought he was going to apologize, so I rolled down my window. Instead, he continued angrily yelling at me; blaming me for things that made absolutely no sense! Shaken and confused, I got home safely and just cried out "God! This can't be your best for me!" The following Sunday at church, he asked if he could talk to me. I told him that maybe he hadn't realized how abusive his words were that night. He replied that he hadn't, then turned it on me, accusing me of misunderstanding him. I was heartbroken! Once again involved with someone with problems.

The day after Christmas, needing to get away and re-group, Miriam and I took a road trip to Tampa for a few days. When I returned for New Year's Eve and went to church, I found him sitting in the seats where we usually sat, but with another woman! They had met through an on-line dating site. At the part in the service when everyone reaches out to one another to say, "Peace be with you," he leaned back and waved at me spitefully as if to say, "She's fine with my beard," which had now grown to Santa Claus length. Three months later, they got married!

Not only were they going to my perfect, loving church, but his shop was at the end of the block that I lived on, and she worked at the other end of the very small town I lived in. It wouldn't have been as bad if there was some distance, but the chances of bumping into them made me feel trapped in my own town.

Like King David when King Saul turned on him, I felt betrayed. Crying out for God to help me remove the pain, I started writing my own Psalms like King David had and sought Christian counsel to help overcome the depression that had set in. I could no longer go to the same church and pay attention to what the Pastor was teaching. Though I knew that the relationship needed to end, i was heartbroken on so many levels; this was supposed to have been a Christian, Godly relationship. God was in this relationship, but now I was out. It was more than just a break-up, I knew that to keep growing spiritually and in my knowledge of the Word, I had to leave the church that I loved. I didn't know the way out this time. I was desperate to hear from God and I needed to hear it in a unique way.

Shaniece, a Christian sister and friend from work, had also just broken up with her boyfriend; we always prayed together. We both needed to find some relief. She told me that there was going to be a prophet at her church in Bridgeport, Connecticut and invited me to come and hear him speak. Bridgeport was about an hour from me, but, I didn't care – I just needed to hear from God, just for me, not a message that applied to everybody, or anybody, just me. This was different than losing a relationship; this time I lost my church, my place of peace and learning. I needed God to tell me the way out of this one.

There were torrential rains that week, all the parkways were flooded, and I couldn't get to Bridgeport for the week that he was there. Shaniece lived in the area and was able to attend; she was elated, and I was happy for her, but I needed to hear him too. Since he lives in Missouri, I had no idea when he would be back. God's hand prevailed. Because of the weather, he ended up staying over the weekend.

As it turned out, there was a person in the congregation who was battling cancer, and the church was going to sponsor an all-day event that weekend, with a parade, a dance, and a service to help; and he would be there to speak again.

"Em, I got down on my hands and knees, and opened the Bible up to *Mathew 22, "that I could speak to this mountain and it would move – and if I believed, I would receive it."* I believed with every promise that God said that I was going to get a word, even if it meant grabbing the bottom of the prophet's pant legs and pleading! I was going to get my word from God!"

Youthful Praise, an award winning, nationally recognized and contemporary gospel choir performed as the sea of people waited in anticipation. Around 3 o'clock, the prophet was announced and came walking down the aisle – like a prize fighter, boxer – energizing the room with excitement.

Speaking from the altar with two large projectors, he delivered a really great message. Then asked, "Who came here today, believing that they were going to get a word?" Of course, I stood up, but was lost in the middle of this huge crowd, with so many others standing. But, he pointed to me and said, "You in the white shirt, I can't see you. Are you light skinned or white? What are you? It was a predominately African-American community. He asked me to come out of the crowd and up to him. Didn't have to ask me twice! It was happening, this was what I had prayed for and needed!

Taking me by the hand, he walked me up the steps to the altar and looked me in the eyes while he proclaimed to the congregation, "This woman is a champion, and she is a survivor. Everything that was taken from you, God is going to restore to you." Still holding me by the hand, he walked me down to the main floor to face everyone, with his back still to them, he started talking to me and said that God was going to give me a new white car. I was just standing there, listening, but it didn't really make sense. God had already blessed me with a black car, and it was in great shape.

Then he looked at me and said, "But you didn't come here today to learn about a car...aaah... but you're not a depressed person either." Then he breathed the breath of God on my shoulder and a strong anointing came over me as he said,

"Because you have divulged yourself in the Word, God is going to make you a minister; greater than the capacity of Joyce Meyers, and it's your life story that needs to be told. He wants you to use this white car to go from place to place because hundreds and hundreds of people are going to be coming to hear you."

I just stood there, knowing that I had just had my prayers answered, my sadness relieved, and received a word just for me and no one else. God really called me to do this and I was humbled. I realized that at that moment, God knew exactly where I was, and He made everything happen. It was God speaking to me through the prophet; God had just called me out in front of over 1200 witness, and as thoughts raced through my mind, all I could say was a soft "Okay."

168

A little shocked, overwhelmed and extremely emotional, I hugged him, kissed him on the cheek, thanked him and walked back to my seat in a daze. I didn't realize it, but he was still talking to me; I didn't know why he or God would be taking so much time with me, especially with all these other people here. He was calling over the microphone to get my attention "Sister! Sister! And you will have that relationship that you've always wanted." That was my heartbreak and it gave me confirmation that I would have that one day.

He continued talking to me and said for me to stand up. So, I stood up. He said, "Run around this place so you never forget what God just told you about your relationship." He made me run around the entire perimeter, around and around and around – every person in that church stood up and applauded and encouraged me. Tears were rolling down my face – and the Bishop hugged me and hugged me and said, "I love you and you're always welcome to speak here." All I could say was "Thank you."

Sometime after I got the prophesy at the Cathedral House of Prayer, I had left work a little early and was going to pick up Beau to go to a concert at Jones Beach. I needed a power nap to rejuvenate myself and I fell into a deep, deep sleep. People have said that they've heard God's audible voice, though I know God is very real, I don't know how to make that happen. During the deep sleep, I heard a lot of clanking – metal, banging against metal – then He started speaking to me. God's voice doesn't have any vibration like the human voice, it's at the perfect speed, perfect tone, and is recognizable just as if you called me, I would know it's you. I knew it was God's voice. He began talking to me and told me that He wanted me to lead His people out of bondage, the way Moses led His people out of Egypt. He doesn't want His people in emotional damage, or any damage, and like Moses, He has shown me the way to do it.

In September I became ordained and was trying to figure out for myself, what now? I trusted that He would guide me through what I didn't know. It took some time to find the next, right church for me. I joined a women's breakfast group at Yorktown Vineyard Church, they made me feel very welcomed. So much so, that I joined the church, but I still wasn't about to walk in and say "Hello! I'm here! God sent me!" So, I listened and waited patiently. The pastor was asking for volunteers to help build a café, in the church; I basically volunteered to do just about anything there was to do.

I got involved with a small group of people to brainstorm on some ideas. But as usual, like everything else in my life, I ended up managing the project and putting together the whole business plan. Miriam was right beside me with her interior decorating ideas and how to make it very eclectic, with comfortable seating for everyone to sit together for fellowship. Though I was still working full-time at a Hedge Fund in Greenwich, and didn't have time to run a café, my heart was focused on two ministries and I knew I had to make this work.

The first ministry, a ten-week cleansing program was supposed to occur in the spring. It was for Christians and non-Christians alike; for anyone seeking the meaning of life; of their life. Its purpose was to bring people into a relationship with Jesus. The second ministry was a twelve-week program that followed in the fall and promised to make a tremendous impact on a person through strong methods of deliverance. Meant to be taken consecutively, these two programs were designed to lead people to Christ and deliver them from their bondage.

While continuing to work on the café, I developed a plan to get these programs up and running. The church supported me and most of the leaders were the first to go through the fall program with me. Though they already had their own relationships established with Jesus and the Holy Spirit; I think they really did it to support me. Initially, it was a bit of trial and error to figure out the right path and method of teaching the programs, but by the following year, I knew what the right path was. What I didn't know was how much I would enjoy teaching the programs and how rewarding it was going to be, not only for others, but for me as well. Because of the people that God brought to it, it turned into an incredibly powerful and dynamic experience.

The spring class started off with a dinner and worship once a week, followed by discussions based on a weekly curriculum that addressed questions like "Who is Jesus?" "Why did He die?" "Who or What is the Holy Spirit?" Other discussions were on how to pray; why we have faith; or why evil exists. You find out a little about each person and what their thoughts are on how creation originated. Some think of evolution or the big bang theory, others are more seasoned Christians grounded by the teachings in the Bible, while others aren't sure that they even believe in God. The diverse combination of thoughts and theories create a great platform for open discussions.

God had told me to be prepared and that there would be a male skeptic in my class. Twenty-five people signed up that second year, and yes, the male skeptic as well. He came from a family where his mother was a minister; he had been a drug addict for most of his life, but clean and sober at this point. He wore his long gray hair in a ponytail and confessed that he had a major crush on a girl at his gym, Amy. He shared some Amy stories with us, and we kind of got involved in suggesting ways for him to romantically win her over. While she was a Christian, he was more aligned with the evolution and big bang theories, but his love for her, and wanting to understand the "concept" of Jesus, brought him to the class every week. With so many questions, I knew he was truly seeking understanding and the Holy Spirit was giving me the right words to explain and provide the answers.

By the end of the course, this man had become one of the most amazing people in the class. He completely accepted the Lord Jesus; understood and grew so much over that course of time, and in the fall, when the next series started, he genuinely wanted to change and signed up.

The entire class bonded that spring and decided to continue onto the fall course of deliverance together; Amy joined us as well. Everyone knew it was going to get tender and deep, and that there would be a lot to go through emotionally, but we had developed such a solid trust level with one another, that it felt safe.

My no longer skeptic and his lovely Amy ended up falling in love. Two years later they were engaged and eventually married. They are now out in the world together, doing amazing things. They're ministering, teaching, working with children, and remain so in love – such a beautiful relationship to watch – a recovering drug addict, sober wanting to learn and share and he did it! He did it! He even cut the pony tail off, pulled himself together, cleaned up nicely and is in a suit every Sunday.

Through these courses, I've become a vessel for God and able to facilitate the knowledge of who He is, in a way that they truly understand Him, and can begin their own personal relationship with Him. I'm able to help identify the places where they got stuck in their lives. Then once they're ready to let go of the issues or experiences that keep them in bondage, they can work through the root of the cause and set their lives free from the emotional pain they've been carrying.

Another great guy, Pete, attended the courses. Adopted as a child, he didn't know his biological father, and I noticed that he didn't really identify with God as a 'Father.' Fortunately, he had been adopted by wonderful people; though he never learned how to read or write, he listened to the Bible on various recordings and learned by listening to the word of God. This man could fix anything, and now owns a very successful construction company. Throughout these courses, he healed his feelings of being orphaned.

We've all continued our relationships beyond the courses, arranged missions to shelters, and we continue to do group studies. The wonderful thing is that everyone keeps in touch with each other. We can't forget what we went through together to get from where each of them started, with whatever burden they may have entered with, to being delivered out of them and set free into the bright future that God had for them all along.

It's impossible to go through life and not experience things that hurt us deeply. Whatever your issues or bondage, the answer is always the same; it's when you are willing that God will reveal those areas to you. When you're ready to repent and understand, that's when He does the cleansing with you. Hurtful words that you know aren't true, are replaced with His truths about you. Only what God says of you is the truth. Remember that. He wanted you; He created you to be in a relationship with Him. That's what makes it work.

Sometimes, I've had people sign up for a class and then change their mind after a week or two. They felt bad not doing the homework; or that it was too late on a Tuesday night, or that they didn't want to disappoint me. That's the one time in my life that I don't say "its ok...do it next time." Because I know that it's the work of the enemy pulling them away from recovering into freedom. So, I say "No. No. You've signed up for it and we're going to get through it now."

Recently, there was a woman that I had gotten very close to. As a child, she had attended a Catholic school taught by nuns; they somehow made her feel condemned. Now in her 60's, she still physically shook from the deep-rooted trauma instilled by fear. She suffered from agoraphobia and feared the onset of panic attacks; appearing distraught in public; social embarrassment.

She lived in fear of crowds, social anxiety; even traveling short distances. Married to her husband, whom she'd known and trusted since she was five years old, yet she wouldn't go anywhere with him. They didn't go to movies, or even supermarkets. She felt that it would take a miracle to ever change that.

In *Timothy II*, God tells us that He *"...did not give us the spirit of fear, but of power, love and of a sound mind."* The root of fear is not from Him. We have His power, His authority; we have love and self-control and can conquer fear and anything that comes from it.

It wasn't until the spring class that this lovely lady really understood that Jesus had been with her all the time and that the fear was not of Him. With her husband safely by her side, she started to come to the course. An amazing student, but she challenged me every step of the way like you wouldn't believe! After the fall deliverance program, all the facilities across the country that teach these programs, attend a retreat in their area. Most of us in the Northeast region attend in Pennsylvania. It's amazing to see anywhere from 300 to 700 people converge on this experience together.

As the days grew closer to go to the retreat, she started questioning things. How many people were going to be there? Would it be okay for her husband to come? What if she had to leave? Would I be upset? My response, "No- no – no – we're going and we're going together!" Then she would ask if we could sit in the last row? Would I go up with her each time? Her fear was incredibly real, and we often ended up crying tears of love together. One evening, she told me that I had explained something that had really hurt her. That broke my heart! I began to question myself; I never want to hurt anyone, and we had come so far during the past few weeks. The doubt and anguish in my expression must have given me away, and as if she could read my mind she said, "Don't you dare stop teaching!" We imme-diately talked it through, clarified everything, reconciled and moved forward.

She had been anticipating all the fear that came with go-ing on this retreat. But she emphatically explained that no, I wasn't too hard on her and that she knew she had to face her fears. It made her feel more secure knowing that she wouldn't be alone. She went!

Her hope was that even if half of her problems could go away, she would be happy. She came back with a FULL, FULL, FULL recovery! She's not afraid anymore! All those emotional walls that had her kept her boxed in and isolated came crashing down. God penetrated her heart, broke them down and set her free.

My father used to say "Don't run with fear! Don't make fear your friend. Don't see yourself partnering with fear or projecting it into your future."

∞

When fear of being rejected – of you rejecting others - or any other boundary that keeps God from entering your heart, you have to allow it to be broken away! It's a whole other way of being free. That's what God asked me to do, lead His people out of their bondage – whatever their fear might be. Get right down to the root of the cause and cut them off.

No more addictions or fearful thoughts, no more worry. For twelve weeks, my group has my full attention and dedica-tion to really hearing them, caring for them, and giving them the word of God to help them. It's a very tender and delicate experience. The last two weeks of the journey feels like you're cleaned up and now you press forward. Life still happens, but you now know how to deal with it and you have a purpose to help others, as well as continue to help yourself.

The night before the retreat begins, leaders are paired up and go through an extensive training program so that they can help those that come forward. The next day starts at 8:30 a.m., standing up front with other leaders, it's no longer just my group. We work with each person that comes up to us and speak with them one at a time. The day doesn't end for at least 10 hours. It's exhausting, but I can see God's prophesy being fulfilled.

At this point in their transformation, the group no longer really needs me to guide them. They know they can now do all things on their own with God. Each year, I start over with a new group and start or continue their journey to deliverance.

The year after I received my calling, my black car developed a 'simple' mechanical issue. The repetitive labor to fix it became extensive and I decided it was time to trade it in, however, the car I had wanted wasn't available yet, so I waited. The following fall, I got the car I had been waiting for, but could only find it in white. As the prophet told me I would, I drove my white car to the retreat and spoke to hundreds of people, delivering them from bondage to freedom.

We are going to get stuck in life, but we still need to get up, get out and live! Jesus came so we could have life – we can't take that lightly! When we project fear into our future, we allow it to get ahead of us and control our lives. Don't make fear your friend, don't run with it.

Over the years, each and every person that has come through these courses, has become very important to me. It's

177

not as if we're just on a road walking from one place to another, we're on a journey together. Before we even start our meetings, I know that God is going to bring them to the other side of the fear or bondage that holds them back. For me, it's just such an honor to be part of their transformation and to see them happy. Seeing them freed is truly my reward. It's amazing to witness how faithful God is in helping overcome our fears and everything that comes with it.

Believe me, there are times that I think that I may be over my head, but I know that the anointing on me comes directly from God and I know that He's leading through me to help His people.

"Jackie, you're still human; you work full-time and have your own issues and life to deal with. Being a minister, isn't easy. It takes a lot of sacrifice. Don't you think you've taken on a lot? I know how sensitive and compassionate you are; I worry about the emotional and physical strain this will have on you, especially given that you try so hard to help fix people and be there for them. You're always there for your friends and your family; for me."

"God uses people like me and that's why I do it – because He asked me to. There are times where I would rather be doing other things, but I'm fully committed because I do love Him and His people. It's something that I will never stop doing. I've been blessed with amazing people in my life. It's important to enjoy life and that's why He wants His people to be broken of their bondage. We're not just waiting for salvation to live in a blissful state, we have a life here to live too. He wants it to be a good life, one of joy – joy through our trials in knowing that He is with us. I'm thankful that I have that joy; I love to dance, and dance as often as I possibly can. I try to remember to spend time with the people I love, and they remind me all the time to do that as well! It's a wonderful balance. That's what life is about - relationships – all kinds."

∞

Psalms 34:19, NASB
Many are the afflictions of the righteous; but the
Lord delivers him out of them all.

∞

I kept God's prophecy with me and He said, "Within six months your mouth will be dripping with what it is you need to tell – your life story." If you knew all the crazy things I've done in my life, I would never, ever have considered being a minister. Though I did them, and hurt myself in the process, my love for Jesus and the way I know God today, and His powerful love is what I need to share. I want everyone I touch, and everyone they touch in turn, to know Him and have their own relationship with Him, because that's what He wants, a relationship – not a religion. I would be nothing – absolutely nothing without Him. I would be going nowhere; wouldn't have a purpose here; I couldn't even take a breath without knowing that it's His air that I breathe. Not only does He keep me alive and going, but He brings me love, He brings people into my life, He gives me everything I need and always gets me through everything...everything...Everything! He says many are the afflictions of the righteous, but with Him, you get through it every time.

There's nothing that anyone is going through that He doesn't know the way out of. Not once, not sometimes, or maybe

– but always. Even when I get distracted, He continues to tell me what He wants me to do, and I keep saying "okay."

"Em, I don't always have the answers or know how to do something, but He gives me great people and support to find the way. Never in a million years would I have thought that I would consider, or even try to write a book, but He's given me you, He's given us editors, He's given us a good accountant; and I won't be complete until this book is done; I know that it's anointed, because of His calling. This is all hard to share, my life isn't a fairy tale, it's very private. But I'm putting it out there, because I'm obedient to serve God and He asked me to be His humbled servant, and I'm honored. It's a broken world and life is so hard and painful at times. My family has had to deal with a lot of heartbreak, from my mother's childhood to her battle with cancer; Dad through his alcoholism; me through an abusive marriage and trials and struggles."

"Jackie, you know our journey isn't remotely over yet in writing this book, right?"

"I thought we had just the closing chapter left?

"Not a chance. You promised we'd find the orphanage your Mom was in."

"You're not letting this go, are you?"

"Nope, how's next weekend?

Though formal in appearance, it was almost welcoming

rather than intimidating. But the backyard was protected

by rusted barbed wire running through wide iron triangles.

Perhaps to keep intruders out; or maybe to keep occupants in.

CHAPTER 22
WE SHOULD HAVE JUST GOOGLED IT!

Life takes us on very windy paths. Sometimes we think we know where we are going, but it's often God's intended destination that creates the unexpected journey and provides us with the greater story.

As promised, like I had a choice, we set out on yet another spring day. The snow had melted, but honestly, the winter still had its hold on the northeast. The sun was out, but the wind cut through us with razor sharp edges. Emel was not in the least bit deterred; frozen, but not deterred. We drove out to Brooklyn to find t he A ngel G uardian H ome, t he orphanage that we believed my mother and her siblings had lived in. Dad had told me that he and my mother grew up together when he lived at 1130 Willoughby Avenue; my grandmother's house that had the little tree in front, with flowers a round it; the home that smelled like warm olive oil when we picked her up. So, we decided to start there to trace out their lives.

Needless to say; that after forty plus years, the neighborhood had changed a bit, but the tree was still there! No, it wasn't as nice as it used to be; no flowers; n ot even a sweet little fence, but it did have a bench made of neon orange 2x4s, with a Caribbean blue piece of wood for a seat. The lovely brick was covered in faded, yellow vinyl siding. "Jackie! You can't just walk in – other people live there now!"

No one appeared to be home and she finally convinced me to

let go of the doorknob and that we had seen enough. We jumped back in the car and drove down the block to the park that my grandmother and I used to walk to. I told you, it was crazy cold!

Shivering with teeth chattering, "Em, I want to find the sandbox I used to play in!"

"Of course, you do. I think my eyelids are frozen."

We walked around a bit, dodging pigeons hopping around on the ground and met Ed, a sweetheart of a guy that maintained the park. He explained that the sandbox had been taken out a long time ago. Despite his efforts, and the city's efforts to keep the parks clean and safe for the kids, people would let their dogs defecate in the box and they often found needles from drug users. They had no choice but to get rid of it. But, he said that he still loved planting daffodils watching the kids play, and when the weather warmed up, families enjoyed concerts in the park.

After a few pictures to catalogue our journey and trying not to trip on pigeons, we got back in the car frozen, but ready to listen to our GPS and head towards the orphanage. It was about twenty minutes away by car, which made sense, given the location of the orphanage to Willoughby Avenue. The expressway runs along the East River with New York City on the other side. You can see the Statue of Liberty and One World Trade Center as you travel down to the Belt Parkway that wraps around Brooklyn, so we got quite the scenic tour.

"On our way home Jackie, I want to stop and have lunch at Carla Hall's new restaurant."

"Who's Carla Hall?"

"She's a chef, and on The Chew; she opened up a little

southern style restaurant. Should be pretty close, we can catch it on the way back."

"You and your cooking shows! Okay, you got it."

We drove through Bay Ridge and Fort Hamilton Parkway, pretty much half the perimeter of Brooklyn! Twenty minutes was more like forty with lights and traffic. Finally, in the distance, the very prominent and recognizable roofline came into view. "Jackie, this is so weird. Until now, I didn't know why I was so adamant about finding the orphanage, but I used to live ten blocks down at 72nd Street in Bay Ridge. I've passed this building several times. I had no idea it was an orphanage; I used to see the kids walk to school."

The Angel Guardian Home for Little Children is actually a very beautiful building. The hunter green, ornate iron gate has "The Angel Children's Home" engraved on it and opens onto a large front walkway that leads to a magnificent front door. The trees were budding, just waiting to burst with their flowers. Though formal in appearance, with manicured lawns and hedges, it was almost welcoming rather than intimidating. Yes, with glass and iron bars, but magnificent none the less. The red brick is trimmed out with white and gray stone accents and in one corner is a statue of the Virgin Mary with three little children kneeling in prayer. We couldn't access the building or the lawn in the back, so we walked around the block hoping for a way to get in or at least peer through the gaps in a gate. Incredibly high brick walls were protected by several strands of rusted barbed wire running through wide iron triangles. Forbidding, and sadly leaving us with the impression of a prison rather than a home. Perhaps to keep intruders out; or maybe to keep occupants in.

"Jackie, didn't you say your Dad used to come here to see your Mom?"

"Yes, they met in school."

"Seems like an awfully long way for a 15-year-old kid to travel back then."

"It does, doesn't it? Let's give him a call."

"Ok, but can we get back in the car? My fingers are going to fall off from frostbite."

"Sure, just remember, this was your idea!"

"Yeah, Yeah! Unlock the doors."

"Hi Dad. Its Jackie, you're on speaker. I'm in Brooklyn with Emel trying to find the orphanage that Mom was in. We're on 9th St. and 4th Avenue, somewhere close to the Verrazano Bridge. She's insistent that we need to know where you and Mom grew up, but this seems to be an awfully long way for a kid to travel back then!"

"Hello Emel. Jackie, we never lived over there."

"Really Dad? But I thought..."

"Jackie, I lived at 615 Evergreen Avenue in Park Slope."

"You never mentioned Evergreen before."

"You never asked Pal."

"Dad, we were just at the park on Willoughby and Knickerbocker where Grandma used to take me; this orphanage still seems like a long way to walk just to see Mom."

"Your Mom was worth seeing. I took the bus if I had the money. If not, I just walked there. But the orphanage wasn't there Jackie, it must have been closer to Evergreen."

"Okay, thanks Dad." "Did you guys write in your book anywhere that I say the Divine Mercy every day at 3 o'clock?"

"Yeah, yeah Dad, we got it - Hey Em, we better write it in."

"Okay Pal, have a good day, call me if you have any more questions."

"Okay Dad love you. Bye."

"Jac, you know we have to go there – right?"

"Em, you're killin' me! But yes, you're right."

"GPS says it's about 15 minutes."

"Ha! This GPS hasn't got a clue about Brooklyn traffic!" When we started out this morning, our expected time-line was about two to three hours; we even contemplated lunch somewhere in there. About four and a half hours later, we were still dodging pedestrians and lights on our way back to Park Slope. This time through town, rather than the expressway. We found 615 Evergreen Avenue. The buildings had been torn down and new ones in their place. Both appeared to be housing projects now, with a sign on it that read "Hope Gardens." Ironically, both had playgrounds built next to them.

"Jac, The Angel Home doesn't make sense anymore. The Convent of Mercy, the parent of the Angel Guardian is only a few blocks from here – between here and Willoughby Avenue. I bet that was where they were, not Angel."

"I agree Em, plug it in to the GPS – I know you're going to anyway."

"Ha! What makes you think that?

Convent of Mercy at 237 Willoughby Avenue, Brooklyn, NY

We drove up to the Convent of Mercy at 237 Willoughby. Our initial research led us to believe that it had been more of a convent and administrative offices for the orphanage, rather than an active orphanage. Walking into the courtyard, it suddenly took on a cold, institutional, austere, almost eerie feeling of a very sad place. I knew this was where my mother had been. I could feel my heart sink and could almost sense the fear she must have had as a child. In that moment, my heart broke for her even more. A very large, also red brick building, but with no white stone details like the other orphanage. There were quite a few windows that had me visualizing the children that must have looked out of them; wondering what would become of them, or if they would ever see their parents again. A sense of loneliness somehow permeated from them, rather than comfort. Towering black iron gates with twisted spiked bars didn't have the same welcoming sense as the Angel house

We started walking through the alley and onto the property when a security guard spotted us. We had our cameras out and told him that we were writing a book and that my parents used to live around here in the 1940's.

"Hello...can I help you ladies with something?"

"I think my mom and several of her brothers and sisters may have been here when it was an orphanage. They lived not far from here."

"It's no longer an orphanage, but they were taking in children during that time."

He confirmed that, given the address at Evergreen Avenue, this would have most likely been the children's home that took them in.

"Em, I'm glad we did this. It saddens me, but I am glad we pursued finding this piece of our puzzle. I think we're done for now."

"I agree. Come on, I know this great little restaurant that serves southern comfort food. GPS says it's only about ten minutes from here."

"You and that GPS! You're buying!"

"Um, it says to take a right up there and then a left onto the Expressway. I think, that's the Statue of Liberty again."

We made the largest circle and ended up passing the park and my grandmother's home on Willoughby again! If we had simply gone ten minutes in the opposite direction, we would have been at the Convent of Mercy at 237 Willoughby. Lunch ended up being an early dinner, but the fried chicken and banana pudding were awesome!

Our journey in life isn't only about the relationships we have with people, but the relationships and memories we hold with places we've been. The orphanage and the Sisters of Mercy may have appeared as a stark or frightening place, but I'm glad they took my mother and her siblings in, because of them, they had a place to live and weren't homeless on the streets. Through all that she must have endured as a child, my mother was able to hold on tightly to God and her faith. Maybe that's why she was able to get through it all and still love her mother, her siblings, her children and her husband.

"Well Em, do you feel comfortable now about writing the chapter on the orphanage? I suppose you will want to research the McDermott castle in Ireland too."

"Wait! What?"

"My grandmother was Italian, but my grandfather was Irish. Mom always told us of a castle in Ireland that was part of their heritage, McDermott castle, but they had no financial means of finding it."

"Seriously?! You have a castle in Ireland? I feel another chapter coming on!"

"No Em, we're not going to Ireland, just break out your laptop and Google it!"

"But Jackie!"

"No Em."

"Never say no – there's always next spring!"

"Love you Pal." "Love you too Dad."

CHAPTER 23
BLINDSIDED

Just when we thought that we were close to finishing this book, I was completely blindsided by the unexpected. Emel called to say that she was coming over to have lunch with me and wanted to have a heart-to-heart talk. I thought that the day would be a bit better having her company, so I started pulling something together.

As we sat across from one another at my dining room table, the sun beamed through the window, and reflected off the crystals on the chandelier; her eyes were soft and gentle, and I could sense that she was really weighing her words.

"You know we can't finish yet; not without including all that's just happened. It's too important."

Tears fell from my eyes as I made a feeble attempt to get out of it, maybe just postpone it for a while. She had been by my side for the past couple of weeks and understood so much of all that had transpired. Deep down I knew she was right; I also knew that it was all too fresh and so very hard to talk about right now.

"You're right, I know it has to be told, but we're so close to the end. Do you think we can put this in the next book?"

"No Jac, now is the right time." I trusted her judgement and encouragement. "Take some time, this has to come from you. Finishing the book can take a little longer; it's okay. Remember, we're doing this in God's time, not ours; only you can tell this part of the story with all its due tenderness and with the love in your heart. You can do this."

I nodded in agreement, "Okay Em, I'll write it."

Over the past two years, I had been very happy working for the CFO of a major pharmaceutical company. It was ten minutes from home, the people were great, and I made good friends while working for a great cause in helping people with MS. In the blink of an eye, my job was at risk. My boss was let go, which put my position in jeopardy. They were trying to find another role for me, but it was very disconcerting not knowing which way things were going to go.

My father called me every day on a regular basis; as always, he was right there beside me, encouraging me not to worry. I would update him in on the steps that I was taking to look for a new job, while still hoping to stay with the pharmaceutical company. Over the next few months, some of our conversations began revolving around his doctor's appointments. Nothing serious, just routine things like a physical, change in medications, and minor adjustments to his diet. He needed to add more fiber and asked for my help in figuring out different ways to get it. Of course, I was more than happy to assist. It was another winter, cold and rainy, so I started making him lots of soups: lentil, pasta fagioli, and minestrone. We added flax seed and more vegetables. Whenever I went out to dinner with friends, I ordered every healthy side they had, broccoli, spinach, escarole and beans, and brought it over to the house for him to have during the week.

Things seemed to be going well at work, I was placed in the IT department, not that I knew anything about IT! But it was something new and I was thankful for the position, so I embraced the change. I was enjoying the people that I was working with, learning a lot and contributing to the organization by creating useful ways of tracking change controls. The project went well, and they put be on their advisory board; I started to feel like things were going to work out. Dad was telling me about more appointments; the doctor wanted him to do a colonoscopy, so he needed to cleanse his system. I told him that I would stop over to review the instructions with him to ensure that he understood everything and that it was done properly.

"Call me tomorrow after the procedure and let me know how it went. Okay? I don't ever want anything to happen to you."

"You got it - love you Pal."

"Love you too Dad."

Several weeks rolled on and he filled me in on his activities: running the senior center, the Bible study group he led that was growing, he was captain of his neighborhood watch, and still leading the AA sponsorship groups throughout our county and sponsoring people, something he'd been doing for the last 30 years. Through it all, he was networking and asking favors from people and politicians that he knew to see if they could help me get a new job since mine was still on shaky ground.

Then out of the blue, he said "You might have to stay with me for a week or ten days if I need surgery."

"Why? Why would you need surgery? I mean sure I can stay with you or you can stay with me, whatever you need, but you're not even sick, so what's going on?"

"I think they found a polyp or something."

"But that's just an outpatient thing." I thought he may have gotten confused; he was getting older.

Mid-March was the twin's birthday and mine was a week later. It was now March 31ˢ and we hadn't all gotten together for it, so he asked that we coordinate some time to celebrate. My sister had started a new nursing job and her shifts were tight. Time wasn't easy to find, but we all agreed to celebrate everything on Easter, so I offered to cook all of his favorites

The following Monday when I returned to work, a press release came out that the company had lost a lawsuit for its number one product. I had no idea that a generic company had a legal suit against us, but they won. There was no way to recover the loss. That very day the CEO painstakingly announced that there would be major lay-offs starting the next morning. Considering the shaky ground that I was already on, I called every recruiter I knew and asked for help.

Sure enough, when tomorrow came, the ax fell, and I found myself out of a job. I had nothing in the hopper, no plans, no leads, needing to finish this book, stay positive, trust God and keep going. To have a reason to get out of bed early and maintain a routine, I joined a gym that morning, then drove to Best Buy in the pouring rain to buy a home computer. My old one had crashed a long time ago and I needed one to job search, revise resumes and cover letters. Everything felt disjointed, things had been going well with the new position, yet suddenly I was out of work. I couldn't afford to be unemployed. I left the computer for the "Geek Squad" to install everything and told them I'd be back in the morning to pick it up. I called my father on the drive home.

"Hey handsome father, how's it going today?"

"Fine Pal. You out in the rain?"

"Yeah, I went to buy a computer; figured I should keep moving, job search and keep working on the book. It's nearly finished, and I still haven't come up with a title for it. Emel keeps saying not to worry and that the title will write itself, but I'm still waiting for God to tell me what it is. What are you up to?"

"Well, do you think you can pick me up from the hospital on Friday? I need to have a procedure done." I could hear the concern in his voice, while the windshield wipers hurried off the down pouring rain. "I have a friend taking me in the morning but need a ride home."

"Of course, Dad. What are they supposed to do?"

"I don't know; something with my stomach, another test."

"Hmmm, okay sure."

"Thanks Pal; get home safe will ya?"

"Yes. I'm almost there now."

The next day, I picked up the computer and thanked them for showing me how it all worked, then flipped the hood of my jacket over my head and made a dash to my car. The rain was coming down so hard, that despite my attempt to hold an umbrella, the wet fur trim hung down over my eyes. Heading across the parking lot to my car with the heavy cardboard computer box, I looked up to the sky and asked, "God, God, where are You? You said You would deliver me!" I prayed that there would be no unemployment since my boss was let go. I had asked that the next job be seamless. I thought things were going well. "I know You have a reason God, but I don't understand this. What is it that You want me to do?"

Opening the trunk of the car, I could hear my cell phone ringing inside my bag. I put the computer in the car and searched for the phone. It was a call from a recruiter, the same one who had placed me at the job I had just lost.

"Hello?"

"Hi Jackie, its Lu," short for Louise. "Do you have a minute?"

"Sure." I got in the car, out of the rain and sat in the front seat dripping wet, to hear what she had to say.

"Listen, I just got the most amazing listing, they need someone immediately. It's in Greenwich. Their products are private equity and energy; the energy piece is being acquired in six weeks. They need a strong team player and if all goes well, after the acquisition, the intent is that this person will be employed with the new firm."

When I heard the name of the new firm, my jaw dropped; this was real. I stayed quiet until she asked if I was interested.

"Interested? Yes!" Wow, this company happened to be one of the most successful firms in the world, of course I was interested!

"Great, can you get there tomorrow?"

Tomorrow was Friday, the same day that my dad needed me to get him from the hospital. I could hear Lu saying that there's five other people going, don't waste time. Go tomorrow.

"Yes, okay 10 a.m."

"Great! I'll call them and get back to you, let's talk more about it later."

I called my father again on the way home to tell him the good news, but not to be concerned and that I would be at the hospital to get him as soon as I finished.

That's great, he said, "God's so amazing." We agreed.

"He can do anything!"

Lu, called that night explaining all the people I'd need to meet with, the culture, what they were looking for, the do's, the don'ts.

"Good luck," she said. "Call me when you're finished."

"I will Lu! Thank you!" Luck? No, I knew this was God's divine grace.

Another rainy day. I put my suit on, took a crisp resume and started driving to Greenwich. I noticed a missed call from my father, so I listened to his message. "Listen, when you pick me up later, stop at the house and bring my insurance card, we may have to bump up the insurance. I'll need you to make some calls and bring my book, they want to keep me here for the weekend."

I arrived on time for what was the hardest set of interviews I had ever faced. Their decision in selecting a candidate was extremely important because they were making it on behalf of the new company. There would be no time to train someone else should anything go wrong. It took every ounce of everything I had in me to convince them that I was serious and really wanted this job. They were concerned that I wanted it because I had just lost my job two days before. Yes, it was true that the circumstances were what they were; I was unemployed. But that didn't mean I wasn't sincere.

During the interview, though my phone was on vibrate, one of the interviewers heard it and said, "Someone's phone is ringing."

"It's mine," I apologized. "It's my sister. My father is in the hospital."

"Are you sure you don't want to get that? Really, we understand."

"No. It' okay; it's just a procedure. Let's keep going please. I'm heading over to the hospital after the interview."

We continued, and I answered everything in truth and to the fullest. When we were finished, we shook hands and the main person walked with me to the elevator.

"Today was hard," I said. "I hope I was able to express how interested I am in this position."

"You did," she said. "It came across. Hope your father's okay."

I drove home rethinking the interview and conversation; changed into jeans, then called the recruiter.

"Hi Lu, I don't know how it went. I did my best to let them know I was serious. It wasn't easy, I hope I did well. I gave it my all."

"Jackie – Jackie, we already got some feedback. They thought you were a strong candidate, that's a good sign. Make sure you send me draft thank you letters to review, one for each person a.s.a.p."

Before heading over to the hospital, I stopped at my father's house and picked up his insurance card and the book he had asked for. When I got to his room, he was in hospital pajamas, looking just fine, talking to the guy he was sharing a room with.

"Jacquelyn, this is Willie; say hi."

"Hi Willie. Dad, what's going on? You look fine."

"Yeah, well they didn't do anything yet."

"What?"

"Yeah, I have to stay over the weekend and they'll do it Monday."

"Why? I'll take you home and bring you back Monday."

"Why don't you see what they say at the nurse's station?"

Storming over to the nurse's station, I questioned why my father was being kept over the weekend and why there was an IV in his arm. They explained that they were hydrating him and giving him a saline solution. I argued that he wasn't dehydrated and that he didn't need a saline solution.

"He's not even sick; I'm going to take him home."

"You can't without talking to the doctor," the nurse explained.

"Okay, page the doctor, I'll wait with my father." I marched back into his room.

"How'd your interview go?"

"Dad, they really drilled me, but I like the company and I think I answered well. I'm praying I get it, but they still have more people to meet with on Monday. I should know soon."

The nurse came back in and said that his doctor had left already but brought in another doctor who could explain what was going on.

"I'd like to take my father home. I don't know why he's hooked up to all of this and why he needs to be here."

"Do you know why your father's here?"

"Yes, he has a hernia and just had a colonoscopy that showed a polyp. Can't I take him home and bring him back Monday?"

"No, your father has a perforation in his intestine and needs to be on antibiotics for 72 hours. It isn't bad and there is an 80% chance he won't need surgery We just want to make sure that there's no infection."

"Perforation? How did that happen?"

"We suggest you leave him here over the weekend."

Something felt wrong. I wanted him transferred to another hospital and started making calls to the insurance company, other hospitals, and my sister, until I exhausted all options. It got late, and everything closed. There was nothing more I could do that night.

"Okay Dad, you stay here tonight alright? In the morning, I'm going to pick up where I left off with all the calls, then I'll be back for you. I love you!"

Saturday morning, I was determined to figure out what went wrong and how to get him transferred and out of the VA hospital. I called every hospital and specialist I could get on the phone, they all advised that he stay put and to give the antibiotics time to work. At that point I didn't have much of a choice but knew that I wanted him to be seen by a specialist as soon as he got released.

Driving to the hospital, my sister texted me that she agreed that something had gone wrong with the procedure. Dad didn't have a tear in his intestine before he went in and they never told us about it. Who were these doctors? They weren't any that we knew.

Ruby, my father's girlfriend and her family were visiting when I arrived. My mother passed away 12 years ago, and my father found Ruby, a true ruby, a rare find. It was her birthday and her family planned to take her out for a beautiful lunch after visiting Dad. She and I stepped into the hallway for a private conversation.

"My sister thinks they did it; I think she's right."

"Me too sweetie, this doesn't seem right."

Peering into his room, he looked happy to have her family there visiting. His roommate Willie was still there, and his family was arriving to visit as well. I walked Ruby's family to the elevator, so they could make their reservation.

"Jacquelyn," Dad motioned me over, "meet Willie's family."

"Hi. Wow, Jack she's really something!" His daugh-ter said. Willie and my dad had formed a bond, army guys, lots of sports talk; two guys sharing a hospital room, no color barriers; just talks of God and Jesus. It was getting close to 3 o'clock, so we all prayed the Divine Mercy together. When all the visitors left, Willie dozed off. It was just my father and me.

"Dad we think that they did this. You didn't just happen to get a tear in your colon. You didn't eat or chew glass. How else could this have happened?"

"Yeah, it makes sense," he said. "What should we do?"

"Stay one more night and I will pick you up in the morning. But I'm not leaving here without a record of everything they did to you since you started coming here. Once you get out, we're going to a specialist and you're never coming back here."

"Okay," he agreed.

Late Sunday night, 'thank you' letters had been written to the people that interviewed me. I needed to make an impact and wrote until 3:30 in the morning. At 8:30 a.m. I called Lu to let her know that I had sent her a draft of the letters for her review, which I appreciated. I needed to get to the hospital, my father had been there all weekend, but I also needed to get these letters out.

"Jackie, I'm so sorry about your Dad, I hope he's going to be okay. Don't worry about the letters, I'll take care of them. Listen, they decided to go with you! You're the one they want and the last person they were going to see is already running late, so not a good sign. Go get your father and I'll call you later."

"Thank you, Lu! Thank you – Thank you!"

When I got there, Dad was all packed and ready to go, but we had to wait for him to eat lunch and have a movement, if you know what I mean, so we had to stick around a little longer. I got the release forms to make sure I had all the records I needed. Dad and Willie exchanged phone numbers, promising to stay in touch. We walked up to Administration to file the release forms and get the CD's with images; all his test results were going to be mailed to us within ten days. We got the prescriptions to continue his antibiotics and headed home. When we had arrived last week, the weather was cold and rainy; but leaving the hospital it was sunny and warm. It felt good getting out of there.

"Jacquelyn, why are you listening to the GPS, shut this thing up will ya? I know how to get home."
"Dad – Dad, I do too, let me drive please."

"Yeah, well okay, put the Yankee game on will ya? It's opening day."

"You know Dad, we do pretty good together, until these car rides." We were back to normal. As he cranked the A/C, I yelled over the radio - his hearing is questionable. "Looks like I got the job."

"Oh yeah Pal? That's great, I knew you would. God's so good."

"Yes, he is Dad."

When we got back to the house, he seemed happy to be home and set himself up in the yard with fruit, his chair and the game on the radio.

"Dad, I may need to start my new job tomorrow, so while it's still nice out, I'm gonna go look for a new professional outfit and call Lu okay?"

"Okay, Love you."

"Love you too. I'll call you before you go to sleep. Talk to you later."

Nothing fit. I needed to lose weight and was striking out with shopping when Lu called to reinforce that I really needed to hit the ball out of the park every day in this new position. There would be zero tolerance for mistakes and that I really had to prove myself. No pressure! They wanted references, and if all checked out well, I would start the following Monday. I exhaled; a week off! Much needed and it was holy week.

The weather was beautiful and Laly was off. She's a teacher, school was closed for Spring Break and I needed a day in the sun. I also needed to spend some time with my father; and I always deliver a Good Friday message at church and needed to prepare for it. Seven of us speak of the last seven things Jesus said from the cross; now I had time to think it through and write my segment. I still needed to shop for Easter Sunday dinner and cook all my father's favorites.

On Wednesday, the Ann Taylor store was having a 50% off sale with another 25% off if you used their card. I was having success building a more professional wardrobe. The sales person encouraged me to open a store credit card to get an additional 15% off. Wow, that meant that I would only pay 10% for everything! It felt like God was saying, go ahead Jackie, it's My favor to you, buy everything you need.

Ruby called and said that Dad was in a lot of pain; that she had cooked for him, but he seemed weak. She needed to go to work, but he was carrying on like she didn't love him. Men - such babies. I told her about this amazing sale and that I was in the midst of shopping, but that I could stay with him all day the next day.

It was Holy Thursday, so I stopped to buy everything that I needed for Easter; quickly cooked a butternut squash and lime soup for my dad; therapeutic and easy on his stomach. We ate lunch together before he headed up to his room for his 3 o'clock prayers. After finishing the dishes, I joined him and listened as he held his rosary beads and prayed "Jesus, for the sake of His sorrowful passion, have mercy on us and the whole world." I prayed along with him, noticing the look of pain in his face.

It takes quite a while to pray the whole Divine Mercy. He intercedes for everyone on a long, long list: for me and Beau, my sister, brother, our family, his friends in AA, the seniors, his Bible group, individual specific requests, all kinds; health, finance, addiction and then prays for his own character flaws and lastly the whole world. I saw and heard his humility. I'm sure God heard my father without him needing to say novenas. My father's heart and relationship with God and Christ is so profoundly real. It is always about the relationship.

"Dad are you in pain?"

"Jacquelyn, I'm so tired. I don't know why I'm so tired. This isn't like me, but I need to lay down. Can you let me sleep for half an hour, then wake me up?"

"Sure," I tucked him in. "Dad, you rest a bit, I'm gonna call the specialist to see if I can get you there sooner."

I already had an appointment scheduled for when the results were expected to arrive, but I wanted to see if I could move up his appointment right away. They confirmed Friday at 3 o'clock. Dad's half hour rest got cut short by the doorbell. His friend Elo stopped over to visit. Dad was already up and engaged in conversation listening to Elo tell us of his day celebrating his daughter's birthday at City Island.

"Hey, looks like our new mailman switched some of our mail, Jack. This is yours."

"Nice!" In the stack of mail were the test results. "Dad the specialist can see you tomorrow at 3 o'clock, we can take this with us. We're going to have to pray that everything will be okay? It's the only time they have, so we are going."

We looked straight into each other's eyes. "Okay," he said.

Elo and my dad were enjoying their time together and I needed to work on my Good Friday message, so I excused myself and left telling him I would be back the next day to get him. That meant a whole lot of driving! Dobbs Ferry to Yonkers to pick him up, then drive him to Harrison and back to Yonkers; then to Yorktown to deliver the message and back to Dobbs Ferry. I needed to manage my time and energy.

He was up early, ready, and calling me. "Jacquelyn, what time are you coming? We should leave earlier in case there's traffic." My sister was calling on the other line. I tried telling her that he was in a lot of pain, she blamed it on the narcotics; but he wasn't on any, just antibiotics. She was listening, but not truly hearing me, he was in pain! With a full day ahead of me, I had no time to waste; feeling drained and feeling a cold and sore throat coming on, I couldn't argue with her any more.

She texted me that she had been the primary care taker for my mother, something I always appreciated. While the gist of her message was somehow apologetic, she was clear that this time it was my turn. Ugh, she wasn't getting that he was in pain and it wasn't about turns. I would do anything for him. I knew she was at a new job. I didn't respond, just moved on.

He was outside waiting when I pulled up. With a baseball jacket on, jeans and a back pack opening my car door. "You got the results?"

"Yeah."

"Let's go," he said. "Did you work on your message?"

"Yeah."

"What are you gonna talk about?"

"Well, I was originally gonna talk about the verse, 'Today you will be with Me in Paradise,' but there was a mistake in the schedule and I need to talk about Jesus' instruction from the cross for John to care for Mary. 'Jesus said to His mother: 'Woman, this is your son.' Then He said to the disciple: 'This is your mother.'"

"John was Jesus' favorite you know?"

"I know Dad."

"This is far, you sure you know where you're going?"

Oh boy, another car ride. "Yeah, yeah, I know where you're just not familiar with these roads."

"Well how am I gonna find this if I need to come back?"

"I'll teach you and make sure you know the way."

The doctor was ready to see us. He reviewed the images on the CD and asked my dad a whole lot of questions. He explained that when the colonoscopy was done, too much air pressure was pumped in. The left side of the intestines in everyone's body is thinner than the right, and that the air had caused a perforation in the left side. In his opinion, it wasn't bad; no surgery was needed. He examined my father and diagnosed that his pain was from the gas, nothing but time was going to help that; the gas was right over the hernia which added to the pain and discomfort. He showed us the images of my dad's stomach and we set up an appointment for a CT scan of the hernia for next Tuesday. That could be done in a day as an outpatient. That was fine with us.

"No surgery until after Easter doc. I want my family all together. Jacquelyn, how will I get here? You start your new job next week."

"We'll make arrangements Dad." The doctor told us that he would be okay and to just set up the appointment and let the gas pass. We left feeling better and headed home.

I drilled him on directions. "Write it down."

"Yeah, yeah."

"Pay attention."

Another car ride home! I dropped him off. "Love you!"

"Love you too, let me know how your message goes."

"I will."

Though I took into consideration what Dad had mentioned for my Friday night message, I wasn't as prepared as I would have liked to have been. Instead, in the moment, in front of the congregation, I found myself speaking of those final conversations that I had with my mother. She had planned out what she wanted us to do. Our conversations became deep towards the end of her life, and we followed her directions. She never wanted there to be fighting between my sister and me. It was her way of saying to love one another. It wasn't necessarily that we fought, just that we were different from one another. I'm more emotional and sensitive; she's more practical and can come across as being hard and harsh. We knew my mother wanted to pass at home and not in a hospital, so together we agreed as a family, to honor every detail of care that she asked of us.

I paralleled my Good Friday message with what Jesus said from the cross when He looked down in His final moments and had a personal conversation with John and Mary. *"Jesus saw his own mother, and the disciple standing near whom he loved, he said to his mother, "Woman, behold your son". Then he said to the disciple, "Behold your mother". And from that hour, he took his mother into his family" John 19:26-27.*

Though there was a crowd of people below Him as He hung from the cross; some that loved Him, others that hated Him, He addressed just the two of them, John, His favorite and His mother. He gave John instructions to care for His mother and to take her to his house. John agreed to abide by Jesus' request, which meant for John to move Mary into his home indefinitely and to provide for her. He trusted John with His Mother and took care of every detail for her care. He also knew that they would find comfort in each other; she was losing her son and John was losing his best friend. Jesus understood the human aspect of caring for your loved ones, and in His last moments, He gave us a word for relationships. A word from Jesus is scripture, a direction with a way to care. A word is our daily bread that we take in that guides us. This had to be so very important for it to be one of the last things He said as He hung from the cross. Jesus is God, but while He was here, He was human too. He knows we need each other while we're here and that we need to help one another; love, comfort and care for one another. He is a sweet and loving God and demonstrated that by taking care of every detail.

Saturday, morning I started making gravy and stuffed artichokes, and called my dad. Ruby said that he was tired and that he didn't feel up to coming to the phone and wanted to know if we could have Easter at his house instead. That was fine, with me, I would just cook everything at home, pack it up and bring it there Sunday morning like I had done so many times before.

Easter Sunday, everything was ready to go, when the phone rang. It was still early, and I'm not sure I was even out of bed yet when I heard my sister's controlled but crying voice over the phone.

"Jackie, Ruby tried calling us both. Dad died." I heard her but felt hollow. If she said it, then it must be true. "I'm heading over there now. I'll meet you there" She said.

Falling apart I texted Emel, it was very early but I needed her. I texted Dionne, Miriam, Laly and be-fore I could get to the next person, Emel called crying.

"Em, the doctor said he'd be alright!" I was hysterical reliving the week. "He was alright! They killed him Em!

They killed him in that hospital! Em! This is my father! How could this happen? It's my fault! I should have done something different!"

"Jackie, I'm so sorry," through her crying and my screaming, "this isn't your fault. You did everything right. I'm coming to get you Jackie, this is not your fault."

"He's gone Em! He's gone! It's my father, how do I go on without him! He's everything Em, everything!"

Dionne called and cried along with me. Miriam called from Florida wanting to arrange car service, not wanting me to drive there. "You're too upset please" she said. Laly called and spread the word. Lidia insisted she'd drive me. "No, no I can do it." Crying and shaking, I made it to the house.

Ruby was sitting on the couch. My sister and her husband were there. I looked at them, then squatted on the floor with my head to the ground. All I could say over and over was "Was it my fault? Was it my fault? How could I let this happen? He was in pain. Maybe I should have taken him to the emergency room. Maybe this wouldn't have happened." Questioning my actions over and over maybe if I did this or that; what did I miss? They kept saying "It's not your fault." Harder and harder I cried, rocking and recounting for what seemed like an hour; continuously reliving the week. Was this my fault? He seemed fine on Friday after the doctor appointment!

"You're going to have to go upstairs and see him to get closure," my sister said. She had been letting me cry, but a lot of time had gone by and we needed to prepare ourselves to allow the medical examiner to take him.

"I can't, I can't, I can't!" Over and over, "I can't, I can't, I

I can't!" I cried, for what seemed like another hour until I could finally get off the floor. Ruby and Colleen each held on to one side of me and walked me up the stairs to his room.

"My dad, my dad, he's not breathing!" Just an empty body."

My brother-in-law had called the medical examiner, while we were upstairs. They were at the door quickly for their examination and questioning. He most likely had a heart attack in his sleep they said, and I burst out that maybe it wasn't my fault then. My sister was in tune with what they explained; from a medical standpoint it made sense. Her husband was listening to everything as well. I'll never forget how he looked at me or his words. "Jackie, it was NEVER your fault." We all cried as my father's body was carried out.

People were beginning to call for Easter; our phones began ringing. We had to start explaining to cousins, our friends, his friends; my son...I needed to tell him. He came over and we just held on to each other. He stood by my side as we moved through the day and the discussions on making the arrangements. My brother and his wife live in Texas; flights during Easter were expensive and hard to find for a family, so they packed up their minivan and started driving with their daughter, little Moriah Joy, still a baby not even three yet; my father loved her so much. My sister and I agreed to start making plans.

As evening was closing in, I realized that I needed to start my new job in the morning. I thought Colleen would be upset with me, instead she asked how I was going to be able to emotionally do that. I hoped they would understand. I didn't have any history with them, they didn't know me; there were other people they liked, and they needed someone immediately. I needed to hit the ball out of the park. If I didn't start, would they change their mind and go with someone else? I couldn't take the chance of losing this job.

Monday morning, I put on a suit, drove the 45 minutes and showed up on time. The receptionist was welcoming and began explaining all sorts of things "I set you up with Seamless and Menu Maven, so you can order lunch today."

"Thank you," I stood listening to her voice but not really hearing what she was saying. My manager came to get me; it was nice seeing her and I really wanted to focus on the job, dive in and try really hard to be present.

"I'll take you for a tour of the office and to your desk."

"Okay," I said. But when we got out of ear range, I took her wrist and said, "I need to let you know that my dad passed yesterday. I just want you to know, but he'd want me to work, that's all. I'm going to stay, so please take me to my desk."

"Wait – wait a minute," she said, "this just happened yesterday? Can we talk about this?"

Briefly, I told her about the air, the perforation, the decisions my sister and I had made. I told her that I knew that they had no history with me and that I didn't want to lose this job. She asked if I needed time to which I replied, just Thursday for the funeral and I would be right back on Friday. A strong family person, she asked if she could give me a hug.

"You are very brave to come in" she said. Then she looked me in the eye and said "We are not going with anyone else. Why don't you start next Monday and go be with your family?" That said so much as to the kind of person she was and the company. I agreed, thanked her and headed home.

Lidia's deli was my first stop. She comforted me, let me cry, gave me food and consoled me. Methodically, next stop was home. I changed out of my suite and into jeans, then met my sister to plan every appointment. Her husband was excellent and organized all the paperwork; changed the locks on the doors, while my sister and I went to the funeral home to make the arrangements for the wake, order flowers, prayer cards, the burial, pick songs for the organist, pick the readings, and plan the bereavement. My sister and I are very different from each other, she's conservative and I'm more extravagant; at times we clash, but we love each other so much that we work through things.

Every so often, both of us crying, holding hands and looking at each other and tightening our grip, we'd tell each other "We can do this!" Once again, we had to keep our promise to our mother "no fighting with your sister." Then we'd smile. We had wonderful parents that loved us and taught us to love one another. It always felt like my dad and I were one person. Now I felt like half of me was gone.

We were so much alike in so many ways. We had the same face. Everyone was important and mattered to him – the way they matter to me. He touched a lot of lives, he didn't have a college education, but he knew what was going on in the world. I wanted it all for my dad – he earned and deserved everything I could possibly honor him with during this time.

There was a day in between the wake and the funeral, so Beau and I met to buy him a black suit. Ruby and her family came over to my home, and we somberly ate the food that I had cooked for Easter. Colleen and I went through albums selecting pictures for the service. I wanted pictures that represented his entire life, she only wanted a few. "We can do this – We can do this," became our mantra. We took our pictures to Staples to have them copied and enlarged; bought several oak tag poster boards; then when everyone went home, I stayed up quietly through the night gluing and arranged the pictures onto the boards.

We all arrived at the wake on time. Some of my close friends made the early service which was a tremendous help; others came later and closed out the evening. I asked Emel if she could come early and stay by my side for a while when it first started; I wasn't sure how I was going to get through the day. She was there from the time I arrived until the end of the evening, and back again the next morning for the funeral.

A group of ladies from the senior center crowded around us to tell us how my dad was teaching them exercise classes and yoga. Exercise class? Yoga! "What did he teach you?" I asked. Next thing you know they looked like there were about to poke our eyes out! In sequence, they demonstrated karate chop poses and elbow jabs. They said that he had also taught them Kung-Fu and self-defense. My father never knew Kung-Fu or Yoga! Em and I laughed; they were so cute and unexpected. But that was my dad!

A few years ago, he had stopped in to check out the senior center and investigated taking some trips, and ended up teaching his version of yoga, Kung Fu, and became the President of the center! Another group of ladies from the senior center came by later and told us about the fashion show they had and how he not only emceed it but walked each one down the "runway." Wish I could have seen that show!

Vinny and Dom, his Italian investor buddies came over

to tell us stories about their stock picks and investment successes. I always enjoyed hearing how my father rebuilt himself. We shared a trading account and he would call me and tell me about a stock he read about or heard about and ask what I thought about it. I'd research it, then we would discuss it and decide whether to invest or not. He had a good sense on a lot of things. We really liked doing this together.

"You look just like your dad," Vinny said. I smiled largely and nodded.

"Jack was a big God guy you know. Couldn't bother him at 3 o'clock; he prayed the rosary and then some every day! If we got there before then, he'd excuse himself and make us wait. Good guy, your father. We never minded waiting."

Nearly thirty years ago after getting sober and leaving alcohol behind, he became very active in AA and was a sponsor to many people. So many people stopped in to pay their respects and described how he impacted their lives. A new person he had recently started sponsoring, a large man that worked for the railroad, was heartbroken and concerned for himself in losing him and his guidance.

"What do I do now?" he questioned, looking broken.

"Always remember everything he ever said to you and keep that with you," I said. "Alcohol is just a tangible item, it has no power over you. Dad beat it because of his relationship with Jesus. Jesus gave you a spirit of power, love and of self-control, use it to take power over alcohol. You can do it."

Another one of his friends introduced himself to me. "Hey Jackie, I'm Sal; can't believe Jack's gone. He was just riding in the side car of my motorcycle last week."

What? Em and I looked at each other and laughed, never knowing what story we'd hear next. All the neighbors from the block watch were there, they used to play dominos in the yard together. It was a steady stream of people, many I had never met or known about; but loved hearing their words about this wonderful man who was my father; and the relationships he had developed over his lifetime; all of which reflected his faithful relationship with Jesus.

It was time for lunch and Beau wanted to take a break alone. Emel took me across the street to Carlo's Italian family style restaurant for ziti and broccoli olio aglio. As we were ordering, I heard my name. There at the table next to us was my dad's very special friend and his wife.

"Oh my gosh Em, this is Eddie; the person who we talked about in the book. The one that took fishing trips with my dad; you know the same trips he took us kids on."

"The ones where he taught you how to catch and skin fish?" We laughed, knowing he never really taught us to catch a fish, yet alone skin 'em.

They were great friends and took lots of vacations to Florida. Eddie was my age. My father started counseling him in AA when he was about 25. Oh man, they loved each other. My father took him under his wing and was extremely proud of him.

"Jack was a kool-kat," he said. Whenever Eddie called my father a kool-kat, I always pictured him as the wild cat on the Cheetos, cheese doodle bag. "Once during our vacation in Miami Beach, we rented a red convertible, but after dinner, we couldn't find the keys. I was freaking out, but Jack didn't worry.

He just said, 'Relax will ya. We'll find them,' and we did. He calmly got in the car, put the top down - you know, wearing his cool shades; and started playing Stevie Wonder on the stereo like nothing ever happened. 'Don't you worry 'bout a thing, don't you worry 'bout a thing, Yeah, Bam bambam bambam bambam bambambambam bambambambam,' and started driving down the strip, not worried about a thing!" Lunch was full of their stories; heartwarming and hysterical, so great to reminisce about the wonderful, eccentric things that were my father.

We returned to the funeral home as more people came to pay their respects. My closest friends were there for the evening service, my church family, my dance family, friends from past jobs, my dad's friends poured in, politicians, his Bible group, AA members and of course my family and all their in-laws. My brother and his wife arrived from Texas with little MJ. Ruby and her children and grandchildren, sisters and family were there; and more seniors from the center.

Such social and ethnic diversity, age, religion, language; all the pieces of my father's life and mine were intermingled in one room. Everyone welcoming and talking with each other. The room was full of love and laughter.

"Jackie," Emel said, "this doesn't feel like a wake. This sounds crazy, but it's been a happy day somehow. There's so much love here no one wants to leave. And Beau! He's amazing, so composed, gentle and loving through it all."

"Yeah, Em, that's how it is. That's what a relationship with Jesus does. I can tell you all about it, but everyone has to experience it for themselves and once you really get it and know for yourself, you're never the same."

"I get it now. I thought I had it before, but I really get it now. Jac, if only all wakes could be like this – a celebration of the person's life. The memories and stories bringing joy and laughter, not sadness or emptiness."

The evening was supposed to conclude by 9 o'clock, we had to practically lead people out, so we could close the doors. Emel drove back home, then drove down from Connecticut again early the next morning to be with me at the funeral. My brother's family stayed at my house and I could feel my OCD kick in. All the dryers, iron, A/C and appliances buzzing at once, blew a fuse while we were all getting ready. MJ, so adorable, wanted to help me do everything.

We arrived at the beautiful church in a Spanish neighborhood, not Italian like my father. Everything was set, the readings and the songs. Having had a relationship with my dad, the priest began personalizing the eulogy. He told of how my father had a vision for Bible study groups and AA groups and what started with just a few people sporadically, had grown to such large sizes. He told everyone that we had picked the readings because he taught us to love God with all our minds, hearts and strength, and to treat one another the way we wanted to be treated, with kindness and respect.

My dad didn't judge people and they enjoyed him. When I really think about it, he had zero insecurities, he was free!

The organ pipes blew while the vocalist sang, "Here I am Lord." I could no longer contain the tears. It took me back to when we sat together at church, with his arm around me. We both sang that song to the Lord. "I will go Lord, where You lead me, and I will hold Your people in my hand." We both shared that bond, we did it, and we meant it; and I will keep fulfilling that promise. The priest asked if anyone had anything they'd like to say. I felt myself rise and walk up to the podium.

"Thanks everyone for being here for either me, my brother, my sister, Ruby, or if you knew my dad on your own. He loved you and prayed for each of you every day. It was so wonderful hearing your stories about your experiences with him. My dad wanted to be with his family on Easter; and he was - in God's way. He rose with Jesus, not just the Jesus depicted on the stained glass behind me, but the real, true living God, who left heaven in bliss, to come down into this broken world to redeem us; He gave us salvation. This life is so short, just a blink of an eye compared to eternity. I thought I had another 10-20 years with my father. I thought his passing was my fault. The only way I can reconcile this, is that Jesus loves my father way more than I can ever love him; and I love Jesus enough to know that my father is truly happy now. What an amazing God to structure life with love and promise salvation for all: "whosoever shall believe in Him" will share eternal life without evil influence. We decide to choose life or eternal hell. My father chose life, God and Jesus; Jesus chose him to enter into heaven this past Easter Sunday."

One by one people stood up and spoke. They came up to the podium, took the microphone and shared their story, all were so different and so touching. Each showing the positive impact he had on their lives. We were way behind schedule getting to the burial, but that didn't matter. What mattered was love. Really, that is all that ever matters.

As we walked up to the gravesite, two military cadets stood in uniform, one on each side of the opened plot next to my mother was buried. It seemed like a mountain of flowers behind them. The cadets saluted me and thanked me for my dad's service to the country and handed over a perfectly folded American flag. I saluted them back and thanked them as they marched off to play taps on their trumpet. Beau and I stood arm in arm, compassionate, humble and strong.

I started my new job the following Monday. Lu was right. I needed to stay focused, prove myself and work hard, very hard. Em, called to see how my first day went; and pretty much almost every day after that.

"Good, very good, professional; I like it. It's challenging, but the people received me well. I like them." I was meeting new people; I'm sure my dad was too; lots of them.

"Jac, I have tickets to the Yankee game this Saturday - 12th row on the 3rd base line, wanna go?"

"Yeah, sure!"

"Great! See if Laly wants to go too?"

The three of us had perfect seats, all expenses paid with waiter service and cheered as the Yankees blew away the Orioles. Eddie texted me during the game.

"Hey, I'm feeling a little sad, I felt like reaching out. Is there anything I can do for you?" Love lives on doesn't it, I thought; bonds remain.

"Hey Eddie, I'm at the Yankee game. Dad would have loved this. He used to record all the games in those books remember? I wish I would have taken the time to learn from him, but today would have been easy. Yankees are killin' em. New York – New York!"

"Oh, you just put a big smile on my face. That's just what I needed to hear. If there's anything you need, you'll call me, right? And if you find any of your dad's AA books, I'd love to have them to treasure."

"You got it Eddie!"

Two months went by at work. The merger took longer than expected and I found I needed to work longer and harder than imagined. But it did pay off and I got the offer to stay on.

Emel and I spent most weekends editing. She had a slogan on her desk. Three short words, "Be Here Now." I'm three weeks into teaching at church and I can't tell you how much that slogan helped me. Every time, my mind drifted, it kept me focused and in the moment.

> Life changes, but we must never quit!
> I have a new job to learn.
> Stories to share
> Love to give
> Goals to reach
> A purposeful calling to help God's people!
> NO DETOURS!!!

CHAPTER 24
A VERY LONG DAY COMES TO A CLOSE

The spring day of a few years ago that had promised us nice weather, ended up being 95 degrees. Emel and I practically melted, tracking my life from the Bronx, to Yonkers and my first apartment with Joe. The sweaters were on, as we started at a place that brought me so much joy growing up. Walking around the old neighborhood, the heat intensified, and the sweaters came off; like the layers of my life that were unfolding. The A/C cranked up as we drove to my parent's home, the house that brought back a lot of wonderful, as well as painful memories. The sweltering humidity and heat broke with a torrential downpour and dark gray storm clouds, as we pulled up to the last apartment that I had shared with Joe. We parked for a few minutes to let the storm pass and then drove out of it. Coincidental or simply God walking with us and leading me through the emotions? At the time, I didn't realize the analogy of the weather to my experience in going back; but now it just reinforces that God was with me the whole time.

Leaving Yonkers, my dear friend asked me how I was holding up. The emotion of the day started catching up with me, but the sun broke through the clouds and the rain washed away the pain. Caught up in the memories, I hadn't realized where we were, and as we took a left turn towards home, my mother's grave site was on our right. I can't help but believe that she was with me that entire day, reliving the memories, hearing my words; knowing that I have always loved her with all of my heart.

Now as I write these final words, what I thought was

clear and etched in my mind, was only a small part of what I had remembered. So much had been locked away deep inside my heart, that only a journey back to where I began, truly unlocked the memories. I'm not suggesting that anyone go back to the places that hold pain or bad memories, but I do think it's important to accept where you've been so that you can move forward in peace. Forgive others, but just as importantly, forgive yourself. We live our lives, but do not need to hold onto pain, anger or regret. We also can't deny its existence but know that God is with us and will forgive us if we've done wrong.

Though my family and I started off with very humble beginnings in a four story walk up; and as much as I tried to wiggle out of playing with my brother and sister; today, I'm so thankful my parents brought them home. My little sister started her journey to become a lawyer, but sacrificed the career she truly wanted, to become a nurse when our mother was diagnosed with cancer. Real success isn't measured by a degree or an income, it's what's in our hearts and how we live our lives that matters. It always comes down to love and what's in our hearts that define us. It's in what we say and what we do. Not just in good times, but when life calls for sacrifices. Sometimes that's what it takes to really appreciate the depth of someone's love. Today, and every day is a day of celebration and thanks to our mighty God and Lord Jesus who made the ultimate sacrifice of His love for us. In my life, I'm the one who has been blessed with my crazy, loving family and the best friends anyone could ever hope for in the world. God is good!

Beau did not take on the negative traits of his father, instead he is compassionate with a heart of gold and is loyal to both of his parents. He's figured us out all on his own. It wasn't easy for me to let him, but necessary. I'm always here for him, and if he should ever say, "Carry You," I'll be right by his side to do just that!

Joe's father, my father, and Shane were alcoholics. My father sought help, found God again, and lived his life sober for over 30 years; he never once slipped, and he continued to help others recover from alcoholism. He was truly a success and the world's best father. Emel's father also battled alcoholism, but he too found his way back to God and became sober, supported his family and remained alcohol free. Duke died an unchanged gambler and alcoholic. Shane proceeded to live a destructive life, lost his restaurants, partnerships, money, and those close to him, including me.

My mother, once an orphan, survived and became a pro-life activist. After coming out of her depression she was stronger than ever and dedicated a great many years of her life to bringing encouragement and hope to others. While running a suicide hot line and helping women in trouble to find their way into shelters, she still loved and protected children in every way that she could. Both she and her sister battled cancer for a very long time. My Aunt had the chance to live a life filled with love, she took a different path. However, I know that my mother, despite her pain, was at peace. She was surrounded by the love of her family and friends right up until she took her last breath. Through everything she endured and experienced, her relationship with Jesus was one that she was extremely thankful for.

My father was, and still is the light that shined throughout my life and I know he's watching me still and telling me to stop editing and finish this book already! No Detours Pal, No Detours!

Memories of my parents are very loving, caring and kind. I was incredibly blessed to have them in my life.

During these writings, Emel also lost her father. Their relationship had often been strained, and she held a lot of anger in her heart towards him. Her father was a good man and had helped many people during his life, but he had given his family a very difficult time. He had always known Jesus but didn't have that full relationship that she had wished he had while he was on this earth. As she held his hand in the hospital and felt him slip away, she felt comfort knowing that he truly was saved as he went into the arms of Christ. However, she still struggled with the anger she carried and battled with thinking that she had forgiven him and had moved past it. But her anger and frustration continued to resurface. After years of continuously trying to forgive him, and through our discussions that forgiveness can take time and repetition, she was finally able to forgive him and turn it over to God.

Now as her mother battles ovarian cancer, though it's the most pain Emel has ever endured watching her mother go through chemo and everything that comes along with it, our talks and God's love help her so that she can be there for her mom and family. No, it isn't easy, and she's struggled with anger and questioning God, but we have each other to fall back on and know how to try and get through it.

Her mother continues to have a comforting, close relationship with God, and in her most difficult hours, despite pain and anguish, she reaches out to God, sometimes in anger, we are all human; but she always goes back to a place of understanding, that cancer is not an act of God, but He is there to help her get through it.

Throughout my career, I have worked with some brilliant people, and formed long lasting friendships. Hard work and a love for finance, lead me to become a Vice-President at a hedge fund in Connecticut.

That's where Emel and I finally met. Though she eventually left the company, we maintained our close friendship. She loved to write and over the next few years, while working full-time and getting her daughters through college, she was able to complete her own degree in Creative Writing, graduating with honors! Her journey was to become an accomplished writer; my journey lead me to become an ordained minister, with a calling to write this book. Who would have thought that all these years later, I not only shared such personal dialogue and my most tender life stories with my friend, but together, we committed ourselves to writing this book and sharing our lives with others.

Who would have thought that we would live through the same family issues growing up? Who would have thought that over the last 25 years, our paths would run parallel with abusive, controlling husbands? We had both celebrated our marriages at the same restaurant on the Hudson River. We both had ownership in the same deli that we weren't aware of until we sat down to write this book. Similar trials and struggles strengthened us as we broke through the bondage that held us down.

We raised our children as single parents and were forced to make incredibly hard decisions to protect them. Today we are both happy, healthy, and still single parents, but blessed with children that we adore and love with all our heart. We struggled financially and lived by a spreadsheet. Our paths had crossed during the most tumultuous times in our lives, and again when we were both financially, professionally and personally successful. After Em left the company, our friendship only grew stronger. Only recently through these writings did it become clear that our lives crossed for a higher purpose. Who knew?

God knew.

We've both been immersed in careers that challenged and required us to manage things that weren't our jobs, or out of our area of expertise. We exceled most of the time and challenged ourselves, but because of those experiences, we learned how to move forward. Everything comes together eventually, we both have that way about us. Emel's career started in the Air Force, then to working for a prominent surgeon in NYC, the CFO of an international music company, and a hedge fund in CT after walking out of the city on September 11th. As for my career, it spanned politics, telecommunications, settlements, administration, operations, compliance, finance, a privately-owned hedge fund, and as a Vice President repo bond trader. We now understand why our careers and lives took the crazy paths that they did. We needed to live through these experiences, to have the relationships that we had so that we could acquire the understanding needed to be able to talk about it.

For the past seven years, my ministry has been one of sanctification and deliverance to transform lives. God did indeed provide me with a white car so that I may drive from place to place so that I can do the work of breaking His people free from the bondage that holds them hostage: guilt, shame, condemnation, hurts, anger, anxiety, molestation, divorce, relationship issues, resentment and offenses, and any lies the enemy uses as a stronghold to prevent them from healing and moving forward. It is my calling to restore them to freedom and deliverance to live a fulfilled life, the way God intended. Jesus died for our salvation to be with Him in heaven, eternally; but, He also died for us to have a life of abundance here on earth.

The enemy has had me on his hit list my entire life, and still does. There is such a tremendous calling and anointing to reach the nations and islands through television, broadcasting and publication to deliver people. He has me in his sites and will try again to make me fall and not reach my goals. The higher the level, the greater the devil that will try to come against me; but with Jesus on my side, he can never steal my joy or win!

If God said something will happen; it will happen. Quitting is not an option for me and never has been. My life work is too important. So now when I ask, "Why me God?" I can look back on life and say that I've seen all that He did for me in my hardest times; and in my greatest times. I have total faith that He will continue to be there for me for the rest of my days and thereafter. This book, my life, is about surviving with the grace of God and through the relationship I have with Him, and through the relationships that He has given me. I could not have gotten through life any other way. No Detours!

CHAPTER 25
BECAUSE OF YOU

Because of You Jesus: I knew You at such a young age; You knew me better than I knew myself and You guided my journey. You gave me the perfect parents, not flawless, but right for me. I saw my father's life change as he lost everything. But I saw him gain it all back and then some. He left us without burdening us financially. He gave me the ability to help others along my path.

Because of you Mom & Dad: You both guided me. Even through my mistakes, you loved me, and I loved you. We each grew closer to God and I watched you do so much for other people. Both unique in your own way, somehow, I turned into a wonderful combination of both of you. My name truly makes perfect sense now. Jack and Carolyn; "(Jac)que(lyn)".

Because of you Beau: I strived to be the best parent I could be and learned so much just by being your mother. I have the most, tender hearted son any parent could wish for. Because of you, we had harmony throughout the years we spent together. You're gifted with an enormous amount of talent, and you brought music into my life in more ways than you'll ever know. You're a joy beyond measure. I pray always for your happiness and I will always love you with all my heart and will always be by your side.

Because of you Aunt Kay: I learned about the Spirit of Pharisee and that religious denominations often use their "laws" to rule lives, rather than showing the heart of Jesus; that relationships can be toxic while under the guise of love.

Because of Joe, Shane, Jared & other bad relationships: I learned that you can't fix people. Their journey does not have to be yours; detaching from negative situations is a necessary and positive solution. Their respective journeys are not over, and I continue to pray for them to change. I especially continue to pray for Joe to accept Jesus and to find healing, reconcile with his family, and to make better choices to live a healthy and full life.

Because of you my sister: I learned that being different means we can make anything work; when we meet at the heart of love. We can do it! We both have so much love to give and we always remain family.

Because of every friend that God has graced me with: I learned to treasure the laughter, the bonds, the memories; the support and love we all share; for our children who grew into the next generation of us. You're my chosen family. So often the Bible shows genealogy of relationships; referring to the son of the son of the son...going on and on. So many names are listed that it's hard to follow, but God listed them because He remembers what they did, and each was important to His purpose.

Because of you my lifelong friends: I learned that relationships are the cornerstone of a solid foundation and I thank you: my St. Anthony's friends from the Bronx, Mary, Anna and Stefan, Rosa, Eileen, Diane and Lee, Roni and Jan, Shaniece, Andrea and Phil, Renee and Lenny, Barbie, Smurf, Dionne and Richard, Nancy and Gary, Nikki, Aleda and Jivi, Victor, Dave, Lou and Jill, Miriam, Jimmy, Rosie, JJ and John Yvette and Teddy, Zulma, Joanne and Ron, Iris and James, Tom

Betty, Louis D., Angela and Andrew, John R., Steve S., Peter, Nancy, Lisa G., the Queens Laly, Lidia, Fran and Joni; Alisa, David and Patty, and everyone's families and children.

Because of you my dance friends: You bring me passion and a special bond that's wonderful. We will all be dancing forever.

Because of you my church family, mentors, and brother and sister's in Christ: I continue to grow through the praise we give God. We pray together, we've pressed into our gifts. We pour our hearts into each other and others.

Because of you that chose to hire me: I learned to make an honest living. I had opportunities to work hard and advance from being an Administrative Assistant to Vice-President at a highly successful hedge fund. I became tremendously diversified and none of my skills have been wasted. Sure, I've had my share of ups and downs through the years, but I stayed the course knowing God was always with me.

Because of you Emel: God graced our relationship and through our friendship, allowed us to write this book. I did not have a clue on how to write a book, but God gave me the perfect person and friend to openly share my life story with and she with me. Our friendship has always been wonderful and grows stronger every day.

Because of you James McSherry, author of _Clean Streets, Happy Streets_: I was given a true friend, and an accomplished writer who helped guide me through this process; one that taught me that patience is very much required when writing a book.

Because of you who reads this book: We can relate to each other. We've been there; we are survivors. We will prosper, experience love, joy, peace, goodness, kindness, compassion, gentleness and patience to endure hard times that life will throw at us. You all have your own life experiences, highs and lows, and people who are your own "Because of You(s)." Who has helped you? Who stood in your way or made you go in a different direction? Who made you stronger? Who do you need to forgive? Who do you need forgiveness from? Have you forgiven yourself? Where has your journey taken you and are you on the right path? Because of God who created you to be in a relationship with Him, you have a purpose and through Him, you can achieve it and live a life of freedom and abundance.

Because of You Jesus: You wove it all together, brought beautiful people into my life. You are truly an amazing God! The great "I AM." Thank You for my salvation and life here. I look back on my life now and see how each person You put in my life has been so significant. Some special and unique in their own ways; others that caused me to detach. But the love You put in my heart as a child of five marching up to St. Anthony's to sit in Your presence; the love You gave me by showing me the dark, as well as the light side of people and this life; the patience You had with me to allow me to live, love, learn and fall, and rise up against adversity – I now share the same love for Your people and Your truth consumes me!

Here I am Lord, Is it I Lord?

I have heard You calling in the night.

I will go Lord, if You lead me.

I will hold Your people in my heart.

FATHER'S LOVE LETTER

You may not know me, but I know everything about you.

Psalm 139:1

I know when you sit down and when you rise up.

Psalm 139:2

I am familiar with all your ways.

Psalm 139:3

Even the very hairs on your head are numbered.

Matthew 10:29-31

For you were made in my image.

Genesis 1:27

In me you live and move and have your being.

Acts 17:28

For you are my offspring.

Acts 17:28

I knew you even before you were conceived.

Jeremiah 1:4-5

I chose you when I planned creation.

Ephesians 1:11-12

You were not a mistake, for all your days are written in my book. Psalm 139:15-16

I determined the exact time of your birth and where you would live.

Acts 17:26

You are fearfully and wonderfully made.

Psalm 139:14

I knit you together in your mother's womb.

Psalm 139:13

And brought you forth on the day you were born. Psalm 71:6

I have been misrepresented by those who don't know me.

John 8:41-44

I am not distant and angry But am the complete expression of love.

1 John 4:16

And it is my desire to lavish my love on you.

1 John 3:1

Simply because you are my child and I am your Father.

1 John 3:1

I offer you more than your earthly father ever could.

Matthew 7:11

For I am the perfect father.

Matthew 5:48

Every good gift that you receive comes from my hand.

James 1:17

For I am your provider and I meet all your needs.

Matthew 6:31-33

My plan for your future has always been filled with hope.

Jeremiah 29:11

Because I love you with an everlasting love.

Jeremiah 31:3

My thoughts toward you are countless as the sand on the seashore.

Psalms 139:17-18

And I rejoice over you with singing.

Zephaniah 3:17

I will never stop doing good to you.

Jeremiah 32:40

For you are my treasured possession.

Exodus 19:5

I desire to establish you with all my heart and all my soul.

Jeremiah 32:41

And I want to show you great and marvelous things.

Jeremiah 33:3

If you seek me with all your heart, you will find me.

Deuteronomy 4:29

Delight in me and I will give you the desires of your heart.

Psalm 37:4

For it is I who gave you those desires.

Philippians 2:13

I am able to do more for you than you could possibly imagine.

Ephesians 3:20

For I am your greatest encourager.

2 Thessalonians 2:16-17

I am also the Father who comforts you in all your troubles.

2 Corinthians 1:3-4

When you are brokenhearted, I am close to you.

Psalm 34:18

As a shepherd carries a lamb, I have carried you close to my heart.

Isaiah 40:11

One day I will wipe away every tear from your eyes.

Revelation 21:3-4

And I'll take away all the pain you have suffered on this earth.

Revelation 21:3-4

I am your Father, and I love you even as I love my son, Jesus.

John 17:23

For in Jesus, my love for you is revealed.

John 17:26

He is the exact representation of my being.

Hebrews 1:3

He came to demonstrate that I am for you, not against you.
Romans 8:31
And to tell you that I am not counting your sins.
2 Corinthians 5:18-19
Jesus died so that you and I could be reconciled.
2 Corinthians 5:18-19
His death was the ultimate expression of my love for you.
1 John 4:10
I gave up everything I loved that I might gain your love.
Romans 8:31-32
If you receive the gift of my son Jesus, you receive me.
1 John 2:23
And nothing will ever separate you from my love again.
Romans 8:38-39
Come home and I'll throw the biggest party heaven has ever seen.
Luke 15:7
I have always been Father and will always be Father.
Ephesians 3:14-15
My question is...Will you be my child?
John 1:12-13
I am waiting for you.
Luke 15:11-32

Love, Your Dad
Almighty God

About the Author

&

Life Experiences

Ministry LLC

Jacquelyn Longobardo

Jacquelyn Longobardo was born in Brooklyn, New York and grew up on the streets of the Bronx and Westchester County New York.

She is a down to earth, real person that by her sheer determination and absolute faith in the Lord, has overcome every hardship that has confronted her. Through her life experiences, she is able to understand the emotional and physical damage that can occur and create bondage that can alter, derail, or destroy lives. Together with the power of God and her relationship with Him, she is a true survivor and champion, and helps others find their way. You will connect with Jackie's honesty and determination as she captivates your heart.

As an ordained minister, a single parent, and a career in the investment and finance industry, she speaks at events, ministers to those that reach out to her, and teaches a series of ministries that bring people into a relationship with Jesus Christ. God anointed her with a calling to deliver His people from their physical and emotional damage and bondage, and to use her story as He continues to guide her. Her greatest reward is to serve Him and to see you live the life of abundance you were meant to have as you grow in your relationship with Jesus Christ.

LIFE EXPERIENCES MISSION STATEMENT

Life Experiences Ministry is a nonprofit organization that has a God-ordained mandate to impact the world. We will deliver messages of Christ and His love for people using the most powerful forms of communication available, as well as the development and distribution of practical teaching resources through writing and publishing books; video/audio/CD and downloadable teachings and articles including media.

We will connect to hearts of a broad population who are struggling through adversity in their life journey using heartfelt "true" life testimonies combining the humanism of practical life experiences with the Word of God.

Our goal is to teach Christians and non-Christians alike how to have a fulfilled life by applying biblical principles in all that they do. Proceeds from books sales & publications, cash donations, tangible and intangible assets, wills, furniture & property will be used for the ministry to establish a facility to host ministry teachings, conferences, and workshops.

It will eventually sow into shelters to assist single parents, abused women, sex trafficking and prevention of infancy farms. We intend to include global outreaches to orphaned children.

OUR STATEMENT OF FAITH

We believe that there is one God, whose essential nature is that of a living, personal Spirit. He is infinitely perfect in all of His attributes; He is the creator and sustainer of all things; and He exists in three persons - the Father, Son and the Holy Spirit.

We believe that Jesus Christ is the one true living God. The Father, Son and Holy Spirit always existed. Each is 100% God in the trinity.

We believe that Jesus Christ manifested himself into Man. We believe he was conceived by the Holy Ghost, born of the Virgin Mary. He died on the cross to pay for all sin as the unblemished Lamb of God, by his blood he has made us righteous. He rose again and ascended into heaven. Whosoever, shall believe and have relationship with him, will be granted his eternal salvation. Acceptance of Jesus is the only way to the Father.

We believe that He has sent His Holy spirit to live inside each person as their personal teacher, counselor, healer, intercessor, advocate, and strengthener. We believe the body is a temple for the Holy Spirit to dwell in those that trust in Christ. We believe in the fruits of the Holy Spirit.

We believe in all spiritual gifts of the Holy Spirit that is for all good. (Wisdom, knowledge, faith, gifts of healing, power of miracles, ability to prophesy, discernment, speaking in tongues and ability to explain). We believe in salvation by grace as a free gift from God.

We believe in the Body of Christ. Each person has a purpose in that body to accomplish God's will. It is our responsibility to spread the Good news, save souls and serve in Kingdom Life principles.

We believe in the 66 books of the Holy Bible as being the living word, inspired in spirit. We believe that Jesus is the word who manifested himself to flesh. The Word of God is eternal and unbroken. The Bible is the one and only infallible, authoritative and trustworthy direction for faith and life.

To live a Christian Life, we believe that God expects every believer to live a life of obedience, in which every area of his life is brought under the lordship of Jesus Christ and the fruit of the Spirit becomes increasingly evident in his life. The goal of the Christian life is to be conformed to the image of Christ. This life is characterized supremely by self-giving love for God and for others.

The life and character of Christ, which grows through the Holy Spirit, is noticeably distinct from the life of the world. A believer who resists the gracious working of the Holy Spirit and fails to grow in obedience is chastened in infinite love by his Heavenly Father so he may learn obedience.

We believe in the Second Coming of Jesus Christ. We believe in the imminent, premillennial return of Christ to take his people to be with him and to judge and rule the earth in righteousness.

We believe in the resurrection of the body. The believers goes to be with Christ in conscious blessedness immediately after death, having escaped the condemnation of his sins through the death of Christ. The unbeliever must face the eternal and holy Judge, who will sentence him for his sins.

He will experience the punishment of eternal separation in hell from the presence of God.

We believe in the personality and depraved character of Satan exists. He is the great enemy of God and man.

We believe that he, along with the company of demonic beings serving him, working out his evil plans through the ungodly world system, limited only by the sovereign rule of God.

We believe that he was judged by Christ at the cross and will ultimately meet his doom in the lake of fire, where he will remain eternally.

If you would like to learn more about
Life Experiences Ministry LLC and donate to our mission,
please visit us at http://lifeexperiences-ministry.com